Humanities in the Time of AI

Forerunners: Ideas First

Short books of thought-in-process scholarship, where intense analysis, questioning, and speculation take the lead

FROM THE UNIVERSITY OF MINNESOTA PRESS

(Continued on page 100)

Humanities in the Time of AI

Laurent Dubreuil

University of Minnesota Press

MINNEAPOLIS

LONDON

The author previously published portions of this book as "Metal Machine Music," *Harper's Magazine,* July 2024.

ISBN 978-1-5179-1904-7 (PB)
ISBN 978-1-4529-7281-7 (Ebook)
ISBN 978-1-4529-7311-1 (Manifold)

Published by the University of Minnesota Press, 2025
111 Third Avenue South, Suite 290
Minneapolis, MN 55401-2520
www.upress.umn.edu

Available as a Manifold edition at manifold.umn.edu

Contents

1. An Essay in Paradoxical Optimism

THIS IS AN ESSAY IN PARADOXICAL OPTIMISM. I am trying to show that AI offers a chance for the humanities to strengthen their relevance and their signification. What would be true in general is eminently so today, when "self-learning" algorithms allow machines to easily "generate" images, music, objects, films, and texts that were often seen as the hallmark of "the human." If we believe that humanistic research is about finding consensus positions, amplifying what others have said, labeling "good" and "bad" behavior, identifying what has already been identified, expressing simple emotions and affects, mastering a standard style, producing balanced overviews and reviews, describing phenomena without interpreting them, summarizing documents or books, or doing passable translations, then this is it. As I am writing and revising this book, in 2023 and 2024, generative AI is already able to accomplish these different missions to a degree that would be acceptable at a student level. I am certain that, a few years from now, the outcome will be more convincing. But, precisely, I contend that many of us have erred in believing, even for one second, that such were the ultimate tasks of the humanities. On the contrary, a maximalist take on scholarship would focus on creation, as a subject and an object, through a differential inquiry into its transformative significations.[1]

---

1. Throughout this essay, I use *scholarship* to refer more specifically to humanistic research.

Let us first rethink how we approach innovation in the broad sense.[2] There are trials and errors. There is novelty through randomness. There is invention, which consists in reorganizing what has been said, but even invention could be broken into diverse parts or thought of as a gradient, maybe with—or without—emergent processes, as there is a wide range between token variations and rearrangements that simply reconfigure the given (its meanings, its values, its consequences). And there is also creation, *poiēsis,* which stems from the boundaries of thought, from impossibilities, from contradictions, from both excess and defect—pretty much where novel ideas and practices arise in the arts or the sciences. Among thinkers and metathinkers, there has long been a complacent view of innovation that reduced this wide range to mainly one type, with the emphasis being put on the incremental, or what Thomas S. Kuhn dubs "normal science."[3] There is no doubt that we cannot create nonstop and that creation is rather an exception to the norm, what I call "intellection" or the extraordinary regime of thinking vis-à-vis the regular order of thought that we could name "cognition." Is the latter the only thing there is? For both theoretical and practical

2. The relation between intelligence and creation or invention was central to the theoretical elaboration around AI and cognition in the 1990s. See, e.g., Margaret A. Boden, *The Creative Mind: Myths and Mechanisms* (London: Routledge, 2003); Douglas Hofstadter and the Fluid Analogies Research Group, *Fluid Concepts and Creative Analogies: Computer Models of the Fundamental Mechanisms of Thought* (New York: Basic Books, 1996). As recently as 2015, participants in an AI conference could show up wearing buttons saying "Mere Generation," as a joke on the abilities of their own systems (see the opening paragraphs of Dan Ventura, "Mere Generation: Essential Barometer or Dated Concept?" [paper presented at the Seventh International Conference on Computational Creativity, Paris, June 28, 2016, https://www.computationalcreativity.net/iccc2016/wp-content/uploads /2016/01/49_Mere-Generation-Essential-Barometer-or-Dated-Concept .pdf]). Today, even scholars who would be otherwise prone to criticize generative AI tend to back away from reclaiming the force of creation.

3. See Thomas S. Kuhn, *The Structure of Scientific Revolutions* (Chicago: University of Chicago Press, 1970), esp. 2, 7, 10. I rely on Kuhn's theory for some key aspects of my own epistemology.

reasons, the majority response these days is positive, and the state of the art (rather: the nonartistic state of the art) in AI is precisely stuck at this level, leaving us with a wonderful device that is also heavily contributing to actively diminishing the amplitude and variety of human reflection, because it principally brings down the noetic to one conceptualization of the mind. In parallel, as long as we will sheepishly accept to be constantly reshaped by the algorithms of social media and by those of bureaucracy, we will also have prepared our minds to be much more similar to the next chatbot, since that chatbot is part of the ongoing reprogramming of human mental capabilities. But there are differences between, for instance, writing paragraphs filled with word repetitions, writing a redundant prose poem, writing in the style of Gertrude Stein, and creating Gertrude Stein's style. Undoubtedly, the GPTs of the present and future can do a pretty passable pastiche of the said—which is why so much of the social parlance, from the *Guardian* op-eds to social media moments of first-person proclamations, are so easy to reproduce with only a few commands to the electronic system.[4] What about the adventure of the unsaid, its performance and interpretation? About that, the humanities have something else to say, something incompatible with the standardization of mediocrity that computerized techniques are able to produce and multiply.[5]

4. See the op-ed GPT-3, "A Robot Wrote This Entire Article. Are You Scared Yet, Human?," *Guardian*, September 8, 2020, https://www.theguardian.com/commentisfree/2020/sep/08/robot-wrote-this-article-gpt-3.

5. I am using the central thesis I unfolded in *The Intellective Space: Thinking beyond Cognition* (Minneapolis: University of Minnesota Press, 2015), see in particular § 1–4, and in *Poetry and Mind: Tractatus Poetico-Philosophicus* (New York: Fordham University Press, 2018), § 1. To some extent, this essay is the last part of a tetralogy also including, besides the two books I just mentioned, *Dialogues on the Human Ape* I coauthored with Sue Savage-Rumbaugh (Minneapolis: University of Minnesota Press, 2019). For my overall argument, I am also using the experimental work I am a part of within the Humanities Lab at Cornell, such as the comparison between GPT-3 and human writing of poetry, and the semantic exploration using natural language processing methods of the French lexicon of race and Indigeneity.

This book is no prophecy. It might well turn out that the humanities as an academic field will soon recede even further, and digital innovations would play a key role in such a demise, indirectly or not. This gloomy prospect is highly probable; I do not intend to avoid it. I am not even arguing for a smooth and peaceful relation between "the tech" and "the humanities," and I am not suggesting that letting be would be wise or smart.[6] Rather the opposite: a strife is unavoidable, and I doubt an armistice is anywhere near, but, in our specific moment, we could see with extreme sharpness what discursive scholarship is bringing to us, why it matters, and how it thrives. My optimism is paradoxical, as it acknowledges that AI nullifies what many practitioners erroneously consider to be humanistic research—I take this invalidation as a good thing—and could concurrently cause extensive harm to its very idea, which would be the worst outcome. At the same time, as long as we wish to think further than the limitations of the given, the impetus of the humanities remains as, virtually, the only horizon for making sense of what we are and could become. By contrast, the one-dimensional narrowness of the most advanced AI is striking. Yes, we could fully habituate ourselves to the pale and reassuring normalcy of computerized outputs; after all, we are so deeply engaged in that direction already. We could even train ourselves anew so that we would become closer to the functioning of our own models, implant more electrodes in our cortices, or couple cerebral "organoids" with microprocessors with the goal of exploring "how a 3D brain cell culture can be made more computer-like."[7] There remains that

6. Contra Lawrence Shapiro, "Why I'm Not Worried about My Students Using ChatGPT," *Washington Post,* February 6, 2023, https://www.washingtonpost.com/opinions/2023/02/06/college-students-professor-concerns-chatgpt/.

7. Lena Smirnova et al., "Organoid Intelligence (OI): The New Frontier in Biocomputing and Intelligence-in-a-Dish," *Frontiers in Science* 1 (2023): 4, https://doi.org/10.3389/fsci.2023.1017235. The history of neural coupling with machines through invasive techniques largely predates our era and Elon Musk's Neuralink; see, for instance, José M. R. Delgado, *Physical Control of the Mind: Toward a Psychocivilized Society* (New York: Harper & Row, 1969). As

the other modes of thinking, the ones that diverge from their algorithmic deployment, show the possibility of, and the need for, an outside to our ultimate transformation into the adjuvants or universal fact-checkers of the brains we shall engineer.

Gabriel García Márquez's novel *Love in the Time of Cholera,* whose title inspired mine, is not first and foremost a chronicle of a certain historical era marked by an epidemic. The "time of cholera" is also qualified by the subjective impressions of the circumstances themselves (and remains in a plural form in the Spanish original *los tiempos*). As for the junction with *love*—like in Alain Resnais and Marguerite Duras's *Hiroshima mon amour*—it does not suggest that the plague, or the atomic bomb, should be the fuel of passion. It rather reminds us that, in the worst times, we can love. The final pages of García Márquez's narrative even show how the threat of contagion could provide an improbable support to a long-delayed relation, as the two aged lovers aboard a ship flying the yellow flag enjoy a cruise that could last for their "entire life."[8] In its turn, the "time of AI," not exclusively a chronological period, is providing a counterintuitive support for the humanities.[9] AI is spreading like a plague. We did not need it to think, but it is there, and, against all odds, we can use its noun and reality to try to recreate scholarship.

I was revising this manuscript, I read Raphaël Gaillard, *L'homme augmenté: Futurs de nos cerveaux* (Paris: Grasset, 2024), a lucid take on the kind of "augmentation" invasive human-machine neural coupling will bring.

8. Gabriel García Márquez, *El amor en los tiempos del cólera* (Bogotá: La oveja negra, 1985), 473; my translation.

9. *Time* is not a word that would belong to historians, and, clearly, this book does not seek to deliver a history of artificial intelligence. The history of AI is, unsurprisingly, a burgeoning field. See, for example, and with different approaches, Nils J. Nilsson, *The Quest for Artificial Intelligence: A History of Ideas and Achievements* (Cambridge: Cambridge University Press, 2010); Matteo Pasquinelli, *The Eye of the Master: A Social History of Artificial Intelligence* (London: Verso, 2023); David W. Bates, *An Artificial History of Natural Intelligence: Thinking with Machines from Descartes to the Digital Age* (Chicago: University of Chicago Press, 2024), a book that is still forthcoming as I am submitting this manuscript.

2. Perspectives and Disciplines

I WROTE *AI*; I WROTE *HUMANITIES*. I intentionally adopt these words to partake in a dialogue that began before I joined in: I situate myself through the reuse of a lexicon, and neither can I wholly dispel its previous connotations nor do I seek to uphold them all. In a way, I am both accepting and rejecting the contours of the discourse preceding me. I cannot seriously believe I shall settle the conversation once and for all. I am aware of the inevitable semantic expansions that will affect the writing and the reading of my text (including misunderstandings, redefinitions, co-options). Through this, I am affirming ideas that are "mine" or, at least, I perform what "I" am as a scholarly person. In all these dimensions, then, what I do pertains to the humanities: understood as a dialogical endeavor where the past (such as a past sense or interlocutor) could be present or future, the process of signification is ongoing; polysemy and contradictions are unavoidably lodged into the most pristine argumentation—the conduct of research neither obliterates its own subject nor transcribes it. This is the humanistic perspective.

This perspective is not unique to a particular division of knowledge. For instance, one could legitimately sustain that a good experimental psychologist should be aware of the trajectory of her line of inquiry, would be open to refurbishing her concepts, and is positioning herself in a collective debate. Of course, but, on the one hand, the humanistic viewpoint is not equal to "the humanities." On the other hand, the scientific perspective (to which the sciences should no more be exclusively identified) is less invested in the semantic openness of the discursive, which is why formalized languages are so central to the sciences. Moreover, a scientific concept, once it is said to be past, is to be done with. There is no use for gestalt or cybernetics in contemporary cognitive science or for phlogiston or ether in today's physics. Their associated theories could be revisited at some later stage to the condition of additional articulations, although they are not readily active the way any humanistic idea proffered yesteryear could again become instantly relevant. Finally, the excess and defect of meaning are often seen as a limitation to science. I distinctly remember that many philosophers and theoreticians see their pronouncements as eternal truths and that the inner fault lines of reasoning have been routinely described as remediable impediments. Such a conception, for being internal to the humanities, has also become autonomized as an axiom of modern science. But, when uttered in a text, therefore relying on the unbounded semantics of "natural" languages, it serves at best as a verbal indication of "higher" truths (the additional layer of formalization to escape the "vicious circle," as in Alfred Tarski's propositions) and, more generally, as a bifid, reversible, deconstructable assertion whose accuracy should therefore not only be rationally assessed but also experienced (thought, lived, expanded, debated, traversed).[1] When chemists Roald Hoffmann and Jean-Paul Malrieu speculate that *"all of theoretical science will respond to its confrontation with AI by developing still further its aesthetic side"*—that is, by emulating "the imaginative power of art" and the crafting of a "near-infinite density of signs"—they posit a consolidation of science (or at least one way to do it) within the humanistic perspective.[2]

1. Alfred Tarski, "The Semantic Conception of Truth and the Foundations of Semantics," *Philosophical and Phenomenological Research* 4, no. 3 (1944): 341–76.

2. Roald Hoffmann and Jean-Paul Malrieu, "Simulation vs. Understanding: A Tension, in Quantum Chemistry and Beyond. Part C.

Indeed, the viewpoint I tentatively qualified pervades the arts, including literature that—like scholarship, though differently— is expressed within the (im)possibilities of human language. Many "professional humanists"—that is, today for the most part, academics—tend to shy away from the inclusion of the arts as such in the definition of their own field. It bears repeating that a perspective could be more easily shared than, say, formal disciplinary training or a position in a university. Severing the artistic reality from the praxis of humanistic inquiry and turning oeuvres into reified documents or mere social symptoms that could neither influence nor enlarge their own commentary is an act of amputation. In 1938, Erwin Panofsky wrote that, in art history, "intuitive aesthetic re-creation," "just as any 'ordinary' person does," and "archeological research are *interconnected.*"[3] The shunning of artistic creation and "re-creation" probably explains how some so-called experts could, apparently in good faith, authenticate the palimpsest painting named *Salvator Mundi* and sold for more than US$450 million by Sotheby's in 2017; it is only by no longer looking at the piece that otherwise-competent scholars would attribute it to Leonardo da Vinci. We should equally avoid thinking there now exists a mandatory research style we have to use in writing and that other poetics are antiquated. Plato's dialogues are plain philosophy today as they were yesterday, although their conversational mode could disqualify them from being published in 2025 professional journals. The thirteenth-century Japanese *Mumyōzōshi* is a text of literary criticism, despite the now rare use of a narrative to introduce thoughts on novels. The standardization of academic prose is just another consequence of the relegation of the artistic in articulation with scholarship. Obviously, the mode of exposition I chose for this book

Toward Consilience," *Angewandte Chemie: International Edition* 59, no. 33 (2020): 13,706, 13,708.

3. Erwin Panofsky, "The History of Art as a Humanistic Discipline," in Theodore Meyer Greene, ed., *The Meaning of the Humanities* (Princeton, N.J.: Princeton University Press, 1938), 106–7.

is both illustrative and performative: privileging the dominant tone of academic rhetoric to convey the differential regimes of thought and knowledge would be self-defeating.

The well-known temporal complication I alluded to (the becoming present of an otherwise past idea or text) particularly opens itself to mystifications we could call, in a parapolitical lexicon, "conservatism" and "progressism." The conversative take will associate the humanities with tradition, seeing the contemporary as one transient instant in a chain of events, references, and books. Notwithstanding, at the end of the twentieth century, the passionate pleas of authors such as Hans-Georg Gadamer or George Steiner, it looks like the hardline commitment to tradition is now relatively scarce in the West.[4] This is different elsewhere, and one could think of the ongoing debates in China about the need to restore a tradition-based view of the classics (the one that had been eliminated during the Cultural Revolution) culminating in the elaboration of nation(al) studies (*guóxué*) to account for a five-thousand-year-old civilization. The election of history as the ruling discipline of the so-called human sciences, very commonly experienced in Europe—turning literary criticism and poetics into the history of literature, philosophy into the history of philosophy, the study of music or the arts into history of music or art history, and so on—coupled with an unprovable creed in the historicity of all things, is just a loose variation on traditionalism. This stance, be it articulated by self-avowed leftist scholars, is conservative in its depiction of the present as being conditioned by the past, the latter being kept and curated to explain, legitimize, and logically contain the former. There is no *now* here, but the prolongation (traditionalism) or the emanation (historicism) of the occurred.[5]

4. See Hans-Georg Gadamer, *Wahrheit und Methode* (Tübingen, Germany: Mohr, 1960); George Steiner, *Real Presences* (Chicago: University of Chicago Press, 1991).

5. On my notion of the "now," see my "What Is Literature's Now?," *New Literary History* 38, no. 1 (2007): 43–70.

The progressives are symmetrically stationed: the past being tied to our present, we have the duty to assess the historical by what we hold to be our contemporary standards. In practice, this option paves the way for a quasi-constant rehashing of the moral, political, social, technical, intellectual superiority of the time we fathom to belong to. The endless indictment of the past (including of those of our contemporaries who are reputedly backward and seemingly inhabit the dark ages) has become a specialty of American academia. It is ill-advised to call this attitude "presentism," as, in the end, it mainly consists in installing everything (but the absolute tip of our current enunciation) in caducity. This attitude is at least as unable as the conservative humanities to produce anything new, for the enemy from the past has to be maintained and even resurrected to allow for an nth exorcism. In this process, all too often, the scholarly personhood that is asserted is usually a reinscription of a socially preconceived category, perhaps complemented with the memory of subjectification episodes. The supposedly progressive orientation of the humanities may seem more accessible to strike an alliance with AI since computerized technologies appear to be the sign of our era. Nevertheless, conservative motivations are perfectly equipped to tolerate a nondialogic recourse to AI in the guise of corpus digitization, data mining, and other automated searches, all shiny gadgets that are tasked with materializing the tradition.

Besides viewpoints, we find the disciplines—that is, modes of organization for knowledge with their own values, methods, questions, training procedures, habits, routines, preferred objects, stylistic decisions, paths of validation, and argumentative techniques. In first approximation, it would be easy to state that the relevant disciplines are only united by their belonging in the institution (schools, universities, centers, journals, publishing companies, the media, economic and political structures of power). We would then assume that history, cultural anthropology, or musicology have nothing in common except their own positionality. The social innervation of the disciplines, set in a context of multifold validation and solidified in a particular organization of labor and production, has a weight on their content, approaches, and motivations. This is not exactly news. More than two millennia before Michel Foucault's own crude linkage between knowledge and politics, Aristotle noticed in the beginning of his *Nicomachean Ethics* that the conduct of scholarship is ultimately tied to what the City would allow, favor, or tolerate. This is why political science, the philosopher says, is the most "architectonic" of all disciplines.[6] One step further, social determinations—I did not say *determinism*—are active in the very training and maintenance of (humanistic) research. This often leads to the recitation of articles of faith that reflect the presuppositions of the profession, or the trending on social media, and are intellectually adventitious. Conversely, many new ideas boil down to the import of other social dogmas that are magically endowed with a groundbreaking function by virtue of their being external to the disciplinary edifice. We cannot stop there. Even if the humanities were originally named and fostered by institutional agency, this would not prevent us from constructing meaning therein and displacing the preset.

Another, less external, approach would define the humanistic disciplinary program negatively, noticing that, at least within modernity, it does not require formalization, quantification, or experimentation. In the meantime, there seems to be a widespread agreement according to which these last three features, separately or, better, conjointly, qualify the other disciplines (now regularly called the "sciences," be they further explained by the terms *natural, mathematical, engineering,* or *social*). This presentation is not without merit, although the lack of requirement says very little about what happens to a humanistic discipline when it uses traits that are associated with indices of scientificity. Is philosophy, if being conducted *more geometrico,* or through logical analysis, or with experimental verifications, a step toward the sciences? Or is it a speculative exploration? Is an interdisciplinary project involving literary scholars and information scientists doomed to separate the quantitative from the qualitative, or to muddle the positivity of its

6. Aristotle, *Ethica Nicomachea* 1094a–b (I, 1–2); my translation.

results, or to dissolve the aim of interpretive scholarship by virtue of using numbers? In fact, experimentation, formalization, and quantification are common scientific strategies, to varied degrees depending on the disciplines, and of utmost importance for their intellectual pursuits. They are dependent on separate, more constitutive, imperatives, such as predictability or falsifiability, that are largely foreign to the humanities. Thus, numbers, formal notations, mathematical operations, or digital computers, by themselves, do not turn a scholarly endeavor into a science, nor do they annihilate the humanistic disciplinary. The latter is rather oriented by aims such as interpretive nonreductionism, the creation of signification, or the exploration of exceptions. Could a scientific imperative be inserted into a humanistic discipline or vice versa? Possibly, but the moment we reject that research be wholly constituted by its social and political conditions of emergence, we imply that, structurally speaking, the differential channeling of the disciplines have their coherence. Therefore, a historian or a literary critic could dwell on regularities and patterns, although they will never be the best at this game if they do not adopt the tools furbished by the sciences for examining such recurrences.[7] Further, they might simply lose themselves if they end up believing, because of the epistemic framing they selected, that nothing lies outside of what their instruments can register.[8]

7. A marked use of the scientific toolkit is typical of Rens Bod's efforts, especially with *A New History of the Humanities: The Search for Principles and Patterns from Antiquity to the Present* (Oxford: Oxford University Press, 2014). His overemphasis on patterns is, of course, a mistake, although Bod sometimes glimpses the additional need for disruptions and exceptions. See: "I started this book with a quest for pattern-seeking activities in the humanities, but towards the end it emerges that the pattern-rejecting tradition is at least as fascinating" (363).

8. I often dwelled on these questions. Among others, see my *Intellective Space: Thinking beyond Cognition* (Minneapolis: University of Minnesota Press, 2015), § 13; Laurent Dubreuil and Sue Savage-Rumbaugh, *Dialogues on the Human Ape* (Minneapolis: University of Minnesota Press, 2019), 125–27.

Salvator Mundi, a painting attributed in April 2023 to Leonardo da Vinci by world experts Laurent Dubreuil and Dall.e.

3. AI Is Us

TO THIS DAY, there is no *"artificial* intelligence," if we take it as a human-made autonomous agent showing understanding and comprehension of the world. Were we to stay closer to the Latin etymology and interpret *intelligence* as the faculty of selecting and linking relevant data (*inter-legere*), then computer science has reached that goal for quite some time. There is a lot of room between these two conceptions of intelligence. The initials *AI,* in between a password and a code name (two letters standing for a noun that is not often fully uttered), register the ambivalence. In this essay, *AI* mainly refers to nonliving machines supporting and emulating mental operations, to the theories permitting them, and, by implication, to human interactions with them.[1] There are obvi-

---

1. In the two volumes of *The Myth of the Machine* (New York: Harcourt & Brace Jovanovich, 1967–1970), Lewis Mumford systematically proposed the idea of the machine as an assemblage of devices, discourses, theories, and social structures. In this respect, the bureaucratic machinery of an empire, for instance, largely anticipates the information technology that would come to be associated with its contemporary forms. This insight was prolonged by Gilles Deleuze and Félix Guattari in their *Capitalisme et schizophrénie,* 2 vols. (Paris: Minuit, 1972–1980). In the wake of such authors, I wish to underline the reshaping of individuals and collectives through the constant exposure to artificial intelligence and locate the solidarity of some epistemic strategies (be they apparently critical of AI) with the reduction to the generative to the expense of the creative.

ous, massive differences between the kinds of AI that have been, or could be, developed. One remarkable point of divergence is about the degree of specificity, from the potentially powerful software designed for a domain, such as playing chess, to the so-called large language model (LLM) that does not really model human language but is capable of varied output, or to the putative artificial general intelligence that would draw inferences from separate faculties.[2] Another concurring and noticeable difference in the constitution of AI comes from the introduction of self-learning algorithms. Would it be left completely to its own *devices,* the machine autodidact would still be programmed to self-train in order to mine the data it was fed. The generative AI that recently prompted reactions of enthusiasm, awe, fear, or discontent couples self-learning algorithms mining human-made data with a myriad of ad hoc interventions by engineers according to guidelines shaping content production ("reinforcement learning" and "fine-tuning"). There are still other kinds of internal divergences, especially with regard to future research. For example, would a generative system endowed with the capacity of additional learning in real time be a game changer? Would a larger introduction of randomness radically modify the calculation process? Would a higher level of coupling between a computer and a living brain introduce another kind of AI? I am not seeking to consider each variety or to promote one type because it would be either closer to a biological model or the most powerful. I recognize such differences, those I mentioned along with many others, but I believe that such engineering problems are not whereon we should focus our attention. The first thing to do is to reflect

2. For a larger audience, a good introduction to GPT and similar models can be found in Cal Newport, "What Kind of Mind Does ChatGPT Have?," *New Yorker,* April 13, 2023, but, these days, both readily accessible and technical presentations of generative AI abound online. *Artificial general intelligence* is very variously defined, with many tech companies currently trying to specify the concept in such a way that their tool would be legitimately called "general."

further on the degrees of separation between AI and "us" and avoid wholly setting apart one from the other.

AI is *not* not-us. We are intertwined with it in several ways. First of all, the "creature" was originally designed by humans, with all their cognitive, technical, social, and political limitations. As machines are now able to code, one can imagine future artificial entities programmed, and eventually built, by AI. This would not be enough to consider "we" had nothing to do with such a production, in the same way the science-fiction representation of the evil robot escaping human control—a tale currently recycled by marketing visionaries such as Yuval Noah Harari—would suffice to exonerate *Homo sapiens* from its own responsibility.[3] Would the mechanical brain display agency, then our own plans, fantasies, hopes, and fears would be inscribed within it, to such a degree that humans could recognize themselves in this dissimilar other. More precisely, the development of AI has been strictly joined to an inquiry about the living mind. While cognitive science originally benefited from the progress of computerization, the whole field of artificial intelligence never stopped relying on experimental psychology for its own tenets. Automated content generators offer us a certain vision of ourselves that looks passably familiar, which would not happen if these machines were operating on a completely different plane. In addition, the large language models and any other comparable technical strategy are, in the first place, a function of their training set. The billions of parameters that the industry is vaunting are learned from immense collections of human-made artifacts (texts, pictures, sounds, movies, etc.). There would be no GPT output of any sort without the records

3. As I am revising this manuscript, the most recent (March 2024) intervention by Harari on doomsday describes AI as a "social weapon of mass destruction," which would be closer to the truth. "Yuval Noah Harari: AI Is a 'Social Weapon of Mass Destruction' to Humanity," GZERO, March 12, 2024, https://www.gzeromedia.com/gzero-world-clips/yuval-noah -harari-ai-is-a-social-weapon-of-mass-destruction-to-humanity.

of the collective achievements of our species predating actual AI. Finally, "we" are, and will be, collaborating so much with our mechanical extensions that "we" can only be transformed by our "transformers." Besides the feedback circuit that allows users to reinject their assessment into the machine by selecting the best answer or the best version they get on their screen, computerized content and processes make their reentry in human minds, which cannot be without any consequence.[4] We can only admit that we are already in the machine—or that it is in us.

Thus, we cannot content ourselves with a simple opposition between the humanities and computerized technology. We are rather dealing with different protractions of the human. The strife I named in the beginning of the book is not the fight of the discursive disciplines against the capitalistic and tech forces of information science or against objective rationality. Furthermore, within the corpus of the humanities themselves, we would have no difficulty finding enshrined conceptions of the human mind or self that are fully compatible with the oblique portrait of ourselves generative AI is showing us. From a humanities perspective, the reality and the discourse of artificial intelligence cannot be perceived as an outside enemy, or as a foreign ally, or as a transparent transcription of the philosophical. If we fall prey to that parallax error, we shall be unable to articulate our own position, either defending a camp whose raison d'être is social (and therefore epistemologically extrinsic) or ending de facto the very singularity of our scholarship. Through the implementation of theories, AI reveals what was not concealed, and everything we do that we can outsource to the machine is in effect secondary in the life of thinking.

4. In the engineering world of generative AI, little actual interest is paid (officially, at least) to the reshaping of human minds. The obsession, in this respect, is rather with filtering out what is called bad content. But the industry seems to be aware of the fact that the exponential growth of automated online content, if it were to reenter the training sets of the future, would pollute the transformers and lead to a dramatic quality decrease.

A postscript. Plato referred to "some ancient discord between philosophy and the literary."[5] Immanuel Kant wrote an essay titled *The Conflict of the Faculties* on the differences of position vis-à-vis knowledge between the faculty of philosophy and that of medicine, law, and theology. The strife I am naming, for being easy to assimilate to societal blocks (the tech industry, groups of university departments), is, however, not solely associated with distinct discursive and epistemic registers (Plato's discord) or with institutions (Kant's conflict). I insist on the transversality of a conception that seeks to anchor the possibilities of the mind in (senseless) predictability, an idea well represented in the engineering sector but that is overly powerful within scholarship itself, where it has been argued over and over again. Thus, the strife could be added to the discord and the conflict that were previously qualified. As for the engaged fight that consists in mapping general political coordinates onto the world of research, it forms another sort of agonistic organization that might only partly correspond to the internal quarrel I am mentioning. Then, as much as anticapitalism or antifascism would like to come in handy right now in opposing AI surveillance, they would miss the mark if they were leading to yet another restriction of the possible along the line of systematic determinism.[6]

A. Laurent Dubreuil is writing the opening paragraph of his new book on the "novel humanities" at the interface of the sciences and humanistic inquiry. Please use jargon.

B. The novel humanities, a transdisciplinary field of inquiry, delves into the intricacies of the interplay between the empirical sciences and humanistic inquiry, with a specific focus on the ramifications of technological advancements on our ontological and epistemological understanding of the human condition. In

5. Plato, *Respublica* X, 607b; my translation.
6. See, for instance, Dan McQuillan, *Resisting AI: An Anti-fascist Approach to Artificial Intelligence* (Bristol, U.K.: Bristol University Press, 2022).

this monograph, I will be conducting a thorough examination of this complex and multifaceted subject, by utilizing a plethora of critical methodologies, and presenting a nuanced and in-depth analysis of the existing literature, while also providing new insights and perspectives on the topic.

C. In the liminal vista where the quantifiable certitudes of scientific endeavor intertwine with the nuanced interpretative frameworks of humanistic inquiry, Laurent Dubreuil embarks upon an expedition into the terra incognita of "novel humanities." This nascent domain, emergent at the confluence of empirical rigor and existential pondering, beckons for a reconceptualization of interdisciplinary dialogues. Herein, Dubreuil posits the foundational premise that the ontological essence and epistemological methodologies of the sciences and humanities, rather than existing as dichotomous entities, can be harmonized in a synergetic confluence. This synthesis not only augments the purview of each domain but also engenders a more holistic apprehension of the human condition, leveraging the computational prowess of the former with the critical hermeneutics of the latter to navigate the complexities of contemporary challenges. Through this treatise, Dubreuil endeavors to chart the coordinates of this emerging paradigm, articulating a vision that transcends traditional disciplinary boundaries to foster a more integrative corpus of knowledge.[7]

---

7. Prompt A by the author. Text B generated by ChatGPT-3.5, OpenAI, February 2023. Text C generated by GPT4, OpenAI, March 2024. One should note that the GPT4 response is giving us an abstract instead of opening lines, one of the many indications that the latest versions of the tool are not necessarily improving.

4. We Are Not AI

OUR COMPLICITY WITH AI IS NO EQUALITY. We are related—but different. As illusory as the claim of total decoupling is the insistent, and false, promise of the functional identity of all minds, organic or not. The brain as a Turing, or as a prediction, machine; the so-called neural networks of a computer; the large language models . . .[1] Nevertheless, beyond even our biological fact, we are not computers. Many arguments on the topic have been put forward. At the level of lacks, AI, as we know it, is said to have no emotion, no consciousness, no experience of the world, no judgment of what is right or wrong. This might well be an accurate diagnosis, even for the most advanced transformer—in spite of GPT's ability, when prompted to provide an outline for this chapter, to summarize for me those very ideas that have been voiced often and markedly repeated in the last moment of media hype about computerized text generators. I do not intend to dispute this list of inabilities, even though I will note that LLMs are quite apt to speak the language of affect nevertheless,

1. Andy Clark has been very successful recently in his rebranding of the mind as a "predicting machine," a category he explains in different places but crucially in "Whatever Next? Predictive Brains, Situated Agents, and the Future of Cognitive Science," *Behavioral and Brain Sciences* 36, no. 3 (2013): 181–204, and in *The Experience Machine: How Our Minds Predict and Shape Reality* (New York: Pantheon, 2023). I had more sympathy for the previous formulation of the hypothesis, under the name of the "extended mind."

that we have no scientific or theoretical agreement for what could be called "consciousness" in humans and other animals, that we also experience the world through culture (and therefore texts), and that the existence of inborn ethics still deserves to be proven.

Another set of distinct features is tied to the current level of generative AI, more specifically. To anyone having interacted with the new tools, four tendencies quickly appear, which have been noted early on and contrast with what we came to expect from human text writers: past a certain threshold, there is a performance collapse (the fragments no longer cohere, entire quotes are being recycled to fill in, non sequiturs appear, etc.); biases are pervasive (originally, the ones coming from the database; now, in their stead or rather in addition to them, those coming from the multiple human interventions during the training session and through built-in rules); events, dates, ideas, and quotes are sometimes made up, in what techies call "hallucinations"; and catastrophic forgetting, when the acquisition of new tasks leads to the loss of previous training, has not been completely overcome. The answer from the makers consists in saying that trillions of parameters, in the future, will take care of most issues. (The same answer is sometimes addressed to the first series of critique, and we know how emergence is being alleged to bet that, in some mythical tomorrow, the right size will be reached, allowing artificial consciousness, or general intelligence, or Ray Kurzweil's "singularity."[2] It is even less convincing.) At any rate, hallucination, collapse, and bias are not exactly unknown to human speakers, as a brief exploration of social media would amply confirm. Another, more fundamental, aspect could be added. There is a very heavy computational load of the deep neural network to obtain just one word or musical note or series of pixels. The amount of necessary data, as well as the layers of calculation, might look disproportionate if compared to human neural activity. The gap

---

2. Ray Kurzweil, *The Singularity Is Near: When Humans Transcend Biology* (New York: Viking, 2005).

would not be a scale issue but a sign that the cognitive strategies at play are indeed divergent.[3]

Without losing sight of all these criteria, or some additional questions about privacy and security, I would personally concentrate on a series of seven other features of generative AI. They are interlinked, and I will appeal to them in the rest of the book. First, the LLMs, and anything alike, are anchored in the past. The training corpus strictly defines what will be produced, subjugating in advance any future production to what has been said. Novelty is fundamentally based on composite variations. Second, the generation model is concurrently probabilistic, conferring a higher value to the ordinary. Third, in this context, neither plurality nor what *I* call "singularity" are performed through texts, images, films, or sounds: impersonal expression is drawn from the reassembling of majority trends in the corpus and the additional supervision of desubjectivized human players. Fourth, integration—such as the consolidation of a general design, the ongoing reinterpretation of the text as it is written, or the overarching trajectory of a theory—is missing from the incremental, token-by-token approach, even when there is no collapse. Fifth, in whatever form, and besides the specific

3. Overall, a good source for the standard list of critiques of current AI is Gary Marcus, who has been very active, and vocal, on different platforms. See, for instance, the book he coauthored with Ernest Davis, *Rebooting AI: Building Artificial Intelligence We Can Trust* (New York: Pantheon, 2019), and his new book *Taming Silicon Valley: How We Can Ensure That AI Works for Us* (Cambridge, Mass.: MIT Press, 2024). Some years ago, Jean-Louis Dessalles offered (in French) a robust and encompassing rebuttal in *Des intelligences très artificielles* (Paris: Odile Jacob, 2019). It should be noted that the industry favors disclosing some limitations over others; see, for instance, the many pages devoted to hallucination, biases, and risks of "harm" in OpenAI et al., "GPT-4 Technical Report," arXiv, revised version March, 4, 2024, https://arxiv.org/abs/2303.08774, esp. 10–14, 44–60, 80–100. Regarding the computational load, ongoing research efforts try to downsize the number of parameters or to distill the LLMs into smaller versions; see, for instance, Cheng-Yu Hsieh et al., "Distilling Step-by-Step! Outperforming Larger Language Models with Less Training Data and Smaller Model Sizes," arXiv, revised version July 5, 2023, https://arxiv.org/abs/2305.02301.

status of large language models, AI is intrinsically algorithmic.[4] Decades of research on cognition in animals certainly supports the existence of an algorithmic brain in living agents. But I have proposed, in *The Intellective Space* and beyond, that automated cognition is exceeded or bypassed through its performance. The creative, intellective capability we can display is not independent from the cognitive ordinary—it overrides it. This is the exception to the norm, the norm where AI is confining ourselves. Sixth, there is, in "us," the potentiality for a concurring plurality of noetic regimes from which AI only retains one. Finally, a text does not contain meaning, it only provokes it in the reader's mind—and may have shaped it in the writer's brain. As for signification, it is locally enacted, while significance is experienced. The text generator just deducts items on the basis of discursive word distribution. The attribution of signification—which is more than mapping, predicting, or extracting vectors—is currently outside of what AI could do. (We, in turn, could interpret the computerized utterances we are being presented with, and one could imagine subsections of future literature departments, for instance, that would be devoted to that task; the novelty should quickly fade.)

On all these dimensions, it is easy to seize how the intellectual activity performed in the humanities could be far from what AI is giving us. At the same time, it is not much more difficult to think of

---

4. My friend and colleague Morten Christiansen disagrees with that characterization (email message to author, October 10, 2023). He considers that the self-learning process ends up evading the common definition of *algorithm* (as a hierarchical set of rules). It is true that, when writing poetry, GPT, for instance, differs from the Eureka machine built in 1845 by John Clark that was outputting Latin hexameters (and similarly differs from the many software that generated poetry in the last decades). It is not programmed for a specific task. This question is intricate, not completely new, and I cannot address it in full here. I will simply say that, in my view, the absence of specificity or the architecture of LLMs do not annul, as such, the prerequired algorithmic structure of their learning, notwithstanding the additional fact that the heavy human-made reinforcement procedures that are found everywhere in current generative AI are also based on simple sets of commands.

countless counterexamples: bland dissertations, lectures, published articles and books that do not do much more than a transformer. Formulaic prose, descriptions of complex ideas with little inter-pretation, repetitive patterns of argumentations, the absence of a scholarly voice, applications of previous theories, self-affirmations trapped in ready-made rhetoric, disciplinary tessellation, or irrel-evant efficacy are regrettably widespread. Outside of the simple, though valid, biological differentiation between our animal spe-cies and our computers, beyond the manifest divergence in terms of implementation, the reason why we are not AI could only be a consequence of what we do—or do not—create.

In its outline for this chapter, ChatGPT is inviting me to reach a culminating point it calls "Embracing Our Humanity" (our words through its own).

A. Write the chapter entitled "We Are Not AI"

B. Chapter: We Are Not AI

Introduction: As artificial intelligence (AI) continues to advance, it is important to emphasize that despite the im-pressive capabilities of AI systems, they are fundamentally distinct from human beings. This chapter delves into the unique qualities that set humans apart from AI and explores the ways in which our humanity, creativity, and conscious-ness cannot be replicated by machines.

. . .

Embracing Our Humanity:

- Reflecting on the unique qualities that make us human and the value of preserving our human identity.
- Emphasizing the importance of maintaining a balance between technological advancements and our human essence.
- Discussing the role of AI as a tool to augment and support human endeavors rather than replace or redefine our humanity.

Conclusion: While AI systems continue to evolve and display remarkable capabilities, they can never fully capture the essence of human experience, consciousness, and creativity. We possess a depth of emotions, a capacity for moral reasoning, and a richness of lived experiences that distinguishes us from machines. By embracing and celebrating our humanity, we can ensure that AI remains a tool that serves our needs and aspirations, while we continue to thrive as uniquely human beings.[5]

I clearly hear the parlance of orthodoxy filtered through the electronic loudspeaker. How far away I wish we were standing from that buzz. We do not have a "humanity" or an "essence" or an "identity" to "embrace" or to "preserve" from autotelic and external "technological advancements." We should not be "maintaining a balance" and attempting to avoid "redefining" ourselves. Quite the contrary, because "AI" is also the unexpected name for a particular way of seeing the human—as an organized, "unique" "essence" to protect from its outside—we can understand that our mental "tools" and all that comes with them are also a provocation for redefining our noetic expression in, and through, the humanities.

In my critique of the generic humanism parroted by an automated generator, I agree with Catherine Malabou that the eventual "danger of machines is human" and that we cannot neatly oppose "ourselves" to our computers.[6] Here ends my convergence with the theses the philosopher introduces in her *Morphing Intelligence*. After years of metaphysical claims about "*the* brain," Malabou, to her credit, finally understood how ineffective was her overinvestment in a biological function of the central nervous system (neural

5. Prompt A by the author. Text B generated by ChatGPT-3.5, OpenAI, July 2023, edited for brevity.
6. All quotations in this paragraph from Catherine Malabou, *Morphing Intelligence: From IQ Measurement to Artificial Brains*, trans. Carolyn Shread (New York: Columbia University Press, 2019), 150–51, except "the reorganization after the breakdown or interruption reinforces the efficacy of the automatism" (119) and "international ethical and legal regulation" (158).

plasticity). Alas, this moment of self-reflection served to install a new phraseology. There is a possible relation between "creativity and routine," as Malabou now sees it, but understanding this link first requires a tiered theorization of innovation. Instead, just as the industry does, Malabou uses *creativity* very loosely to refer to strategies at playing go (as evaluated by "experts") along with apparently any production in "music, painting, literature." This conceptual fuzziness culminates in an assessment of computerized forms that would not sound exotic in a tech seminar sponsored by Meta: "Their creativity is boundless." Of course, "they" are pretty heavily bounded by their programs. Then, declaring that "algorithmic calculation . . . is capable of simulating noncalculation" is either nonsensical or ungenuine. The incomputable is simply not computable by a computer, and no "simulation" can alter this. Thus, thinking may be unequal to calculating, and there is no "*automatic creation*," strictly speaking, but, at best, automated invention. Moreover, I would not exemplify "qualitative" "noncalculation" with "spontaneity" and "the directness of emotions," as these are cognitive processes. In the end, Malabou enchains the noetic to the figure of "automatism," further stating that "the reorganization after the breakdown or interruption reinforces the efficacy of the automatism," which paves the way to "the reduction of human genius to a series of algorithms." Except that there was no equation such as *brain plasticity equals human genius equals inventiveness equals qualitative equals spontaneity* to begin with. As for mental routines, they are also routinely reorganized, and it is arbitrary to suppose that their pruning and consolidation (plasticity) are necessarily a "dialectical" effect of creativity. The last word given to the *Aufhebung* in "automatism" clearly situates Malabou's plane of intervention, a gauche postmodern humanism being replaced by the diffuse conflation of all intelligences, under the watch of "international ethical and legal regulation." This will not be where I'll go.

5. Naming the Human(ities)

HERE IS A COMMON MISCONCEPTION, and I sometimes feel I had to fight it my entire scholarly life. The fact that a noun or a phrase would be selected to yield meaning more readily does not entail that words encapsulate and, even less so, create semantics. In particular, the absence of a term in a given vocabulary shows that the relevant group of speakers does not feel a need to lexicalize; this does not prove the absence of signification, even at the juncture of social institutions. Contrary to what is argued here and there, the recourse to "the humanities" as an academic category in American universities does not at all entail that this grouping is only "an effect of a particular time and world."[1] The currency of the locution in the United States today is the mark of a specific social-historical development and embedding within political structures; but it is not an "effect." Rushed inferences serve to diminish scholarship. As much as we could justifiably speak of "the humanities" in contexts that are historically and culturally distant from modern American academia if we do not apply a preconceived understanding of them, we could also dispose of the expression. This

---

1. Paul Reitter and Chad Wellmon, *Permanent Crisis: The Humanities in a Disenchanted Age* (Chicago: University of Chicago Press, 2021), 260. See also, among many others, Geoffrey Galt Harpham, *The Humanities and the Dream of America* (Chicago: University of Chicago Press, 2011), 8.

essay could be rewritten using terms other than *the humanities* and, retaining its significance, through different meanings.

For instance, one could speak of the "science of the mind" (in German, *Geisteswissenschaft*), or of "letters" (in French, *lettres*), or of "human writings and culture" (in Chinese, *rénwén*), or of "liberal arts" (in Latin, *artes liberales*).[2] I sometimes use these phrases in this book, as nonoverlapping equivalents, to which I add other expressions, such as "the discursive disciplines." Each time, the task is not only to acknowledge the preconditioned semantics such utterances convey but also to modify the understanding of the given. *The humanities*, here, are never "the humanities," as if everybody knew what they were and naturally agreed on their definition. If such were the case, there would be no place for the strife I have mentioned. And similarly for all other synonyms, all of them being inserted in a setting but being equally capable of reaching further—each time, however, the mark of this setting conjures up an aspect, a form, a contour that should not be a terminus ad quem but a quo. If I write "the discursive disciplines," I am focusing through the second term on the epistemic dimension, notwithstanding the possibility of a perspective or of an idea that would go beyond the established branches of knowledge. With the adjective *discursive*, I insist on a certain use of human verbal language that is running its course (*dis-cursus*) or is in flux, thereby apt to exacerbate its own signification, and in contradistinction with mathematical notations and all positions on stylistic transparency that equate writing with a direct

2. About *Geisteswissenschaft*, see, for example, Wilhelm Dilthey, *Gesammelte Schriften*, vol. 1, *Einleitung in die Geisteswissenschaften* (Leipzig, Germany: Teubner, 1922); about *lettres*, Georges Gusdorf, *Les sciences humaines et la pensée occidentale*, vol. 1, *De l'histoire des sciences à l'histoire de la pensée* (Paris: Payot, 1966), esp. 10–33; about *rénwén*, Yu-yu Cheng, "The Origins of *Wen* in the Chinese Tradition," trans. Emily Sun, *Yearbook of Comparative Literature* 57 (2011): 189–212; about *artes liberales*, Friedmar Kühnert, *Allgemeinbildung und Fachbildung in der Antike* (Berlin: Akademie, 1961), and Michael Stolz, *Artes-liberales-Zyklen* (Tübingen, Germany: Franke, 2004).

script or dictation of mental concepts (what logician Gottlob Frege called *Begriffsschrift*), another constituent of the AI agenda within reflexive theory.[3] It also reminds us that we are working *in* language. Were we to speak of *Geisteswissenschaften,* we would relate scholarship to noetic activity and face the validity of the computer as a model of mental activity. The ensuing opposition between the sciences of the mind and the natural sciences (*Naturwissenschaften*) is immediately becoming dubious to us, if the distinction serves to extract the human mind from the rest of nature, which is nothing more than a parochial, theological view. As for artificial intelligence itself, it would seem to be a product, based on methods perfected in the sciences of nature, that would fall into an inquiry about the mind, being granted that the spiritual connotation of *Geist* almost spontaneously hints at the ghost in the machine. When I refer to *artes liberales,* I stress the emancipatory dimension of a certain sort of liberating knowledge. There, the next question would concern the place and role of the formalized and experimental sciences, traditionally included, at least in part, in the liberal arts. Alternatively, I could use *letters,* a term that is not restricted to the alphabetic but signals a form of writing within writing (as "letters" are not understandable as all books and manuscripts), a plurality, as well as a literary becoming. While it is certain that the appellation *lettres,* in French, was tied to the reformation of the university under Napoléon (with the instauration of the "faculty of letters," alongside those of "medicine," "law," and "sciences," and the consecutive divisions in secondary education or at the École normale supérieure), its potential is vaster: it exhibits the stratified use of language in scholarship and a possible influence—within knowledge itself—of the literary, understood as the warrant of signification, and of the differential poetics of the disciplines.

3. A term Frege himself glossed as the "'formal language of pure thought'" in his *Begriffsschrift* (Halle, Germany: Nebert, 1879), x and subtitle; my translation.

In this lexicon, *the humane letters,* just like *rénwén* in Chinese, have the particularity of enunciating what looks like a human core. Is it humanism? And, if yes, which one? Does this matter as we consider artificial intelligence? *Humanism* is largely a word coined by nineteenth-century historians to render what they perceived to be an intellectual renaissance, often said to begin with Petrarch.[4] The novelty of the term, in its own turn, does not rule out its relevance to addressing transformations occurring in the fourteenth century or before. Then, one finds in Cicero and, right before him, in Scipio Africanus's circle the repeated invocation of *humanitas* for a combination of education and scholarship with some cultured, civilized benevolence.[5] A banal understanding of this appeal to the human by the very name of the humanities (or to *rén* in *rénwén*) would put at their center a predefined conception of what "we" are, as well as the mission to laud, like, or protect humankind (GPT's imperative to "embrace our humanity"). Notably, the oldest mention of *rénwén,* in the *Yijing,* has a manifestly different acceptation that one could say has been later co-opted as a Chinese equivalent for the humane letters. *Wén* could stand for *culture,* to an extent; it is an inscription, an adornment, a writing. From the *Yijing* to Mencius, *rénwén* is contrasted with *tiānwén,* the mark of the (divine) heaven.[6] Ancient

---

4. See, e.g., Richard Claverhouse Jebb, *Humanism in Education* (London: Macmillan, 1899), 5–6; Rudolf Pfeiffer, *History of Classical Scholarship: From 1300 to 1850* (Oxford: Clarendon Press, 1976), 15–16; Anthony Grafton and David Bell, *The West: A New History* (New York: Norton, 2018), 356–57.

5. A still-relevant history could be found in Oscar E. Nybakken, "Humanitas Romana," *Transactions and Proceedings of the American Philological Association* 70 (1939): 396–413.

6. *Yijing* [Book of Changes], 22; *Mencius,* I, 3. See also Xiaoyue Xu, *Essentials of Chinese Humanism: Confucianism, Daoism, and Buddhism,* trans. Zhen Chi (n.p.: Bridge21, 2023), 8–10. Differences often supposed to exist along an East–West divide between the conceptions of *rénwén* and of *humanities* (such as the inclusion, or exclusion, of the arts, or the link, or lack thereof, between scholarship and morality) do not, in fact, typify China versus Europe.

Greek occurrences of *anthrōpinos* or *anthrōpeios* (*human*) in an epistemic situation equally articulate the terms with the vocabulary of the divine.[7] In such corpora, Chinese or Greek, the human affairs are negatively determined, essentially, by their upper boundary (the divine). They do not arise from the stipulated characteristics or dignity that the disciplines of culture should exemplify, mirror, or consolidate—another, concurring, interpretation of the human supposition within the humanities. Besides these negative and positive determinations is a third conception we would call "human," in a particular and nonbiological sense—that which is shaped by the humanistic viewpoint. Humanness would not be a factual positionality or an essence but a becoming (thus, not a datum), a gradient. I have more sympathy for this latter approach, to be found from the ancient Romans to Renaissance scholars to contemporary radical Black thought.[8] It also allows for members of other species, such as the bonobo Kanzi, to become "human," in his way and under the condition of dialogue.[9] It may point toward the particularities of self-cultivation through an immersion within the worlds of letters. It even, tangentially, makes room, within the process of humanization, for AI, although clearly not under its current manifestations.

Nonetheless, one should not conceal that any qualification of the human in the humanities is opening the possibility of undue exclusion. The negative definition easily introduces religious ordering, banning nonbelievers; the positive determination repeatedly served

7. See, e.g., Menander, *Sententiæ* 1; Strabo, *Geographica* I, i, 1; Sextus Empiricus, *Adversus mathematicos* IX, 13.

8. See, for instance, Aulus Gellius, *Noctes Atticæ* XIII, 17; Giovanni Pico della Mirandola, *De hominis dignitate* (Rome: Atanòr, 1986), 79 (1485 letter to Ermolao Barbaro); Fred Moten, *Consent Not to Be a Single Being*, vol. 1, *Black and Blur* (Durham, N.C.: Duke University Press, 2017), 217.

9. See especially Laurent Dubreuil and Sue Savage-Rumbaugh, *Dialogues on the Human Ape* (Minneapolis: University of Minnesota Press, 2019), 68–85. In a vast bibliography, I am noting Arnaud Gerspacher, *The Owls Are Not What They Seem: Artist as Ethologist* (Minneapolis: University of Minnesota Press, 2022).

to dehumanize people perceived to be barbarians, Indigenous, Black, or "of color," and still sustains the structural relegation of (other) animals into one category; the postpositional interpretation entails that if we could become more human, then some of "us" are less so, which resonates too quickly with other hierarchical systems of domination. Because of that, one could be tempted to abandon the jargon of the humanities altogether. Still, the very intricacy of the category, its multifold and perilous semantics, might be better decided by renewed inquiry than by principled erasure. At any rate, labels such as "posthumanities" would not suffice to alleviate concerns, especially if they were to espouse AI in general, as a way to bypass traditionalist (positive) "humanism."[10] Whatever lexicon we will opt for, we will have to problematize our own discourse, which, after all, is also what letters are for.

A. Ultimately, whether or not AI is "divine" is a matter of personal belief . . .

B. But what is your personal belief on the matter?

A. My personal belief is that AI is not divine in the traditional sense. . . . I believe that the relationship between AI and divinity is a complex one. It is a topic that is likely to be debated for many years to come. I am excited to see how this relationship develops in the future.[11]

10. On this term, see the now classical book by Cary Wolfe, *What Is Posthumanism?* (Minneapolis: University of Minnesota Press, 2009). For my take on this category, see *The Intellective Space: Thinking beyond Cognition* (Minneapolis: University of Minnesota Press, 2015), § 89.

11. Texts A generated by Bard, Google, July 2023, edited for brevity. Prompt B provided by the author.

6. The Ongoing Reprogramming

THE EFFICACY OF AI CONTRIBUTES to the dissemination and apparent confirmation of the doctrines it stems from. This is how we came to speak of *techno-logy,* whose suffix should reserve the word to a study or a discourse; this is a philological mistake but a philosophical assertion—computerized techniques are implementing a dogmatic program. Without uttering a word, AI was telling us what we should do and be; now that it "speaks," profusely, its indications are louder. Aside from a very well-orchestrated PR campaign, why was there in 2023 such an overwhelming reaction, especially in the United States, to the circulation of a few cherry-picked texts outputted by ChatGPT? Were these fragments brilliant, original, meaningful, significant, beautiful? Not really, but our collective habituation to mediocrity and our intellectual numbness undoubtedly prepared us to be more receptive to the onslaught of automated completions. At this stage, virtually none of them would strike us as being remotely "intelligent" if we had not already contributed to our reprogramming. Generative systems are another step down a road we took some time ago. In particular, the globalized technologies of communication constantly downsize and colonize our noetic space.

The ordering of computerized exchange, instant response, status updates, and other electronic buzz first destroys focus. Multitasking, for instance, is a lure, and repeated experiments have established that the more we divide our attention when pursuing even simple media activities, the looser we are in terms of performance and the

happier we feel about ourselves and our failing abilities.[1] Along with
our divided attention, the stream of connection and disconnection
we subject ourselves to when answering a dubiously urgent email,
checking a post on a social network or the news, and picking up the
phone makes it almost impossible to be durably immersed in high-
level mental occupations. The objectifying stream goes against the
subjective flow.[2] If we no longer have the experience of being lost in
a book or a movie, we are missing what thinking and the arts could
procure—not only a temporary subtraction from this world and an
associated elation (alcohol and entertainment would provide as
much) but also the means to bring something back from this trip,
something that will change us and make our lives more livable. This
differs from the algorithmic machinery of "social" media and the
brain addictions it fosters. The electronic and communicational
sphere is, indeed, a mode of direct intervention on the working of
our minds. Its, oft-neglected, physical infrastructure pollutes the
environment and wastes resources to an amazing degree. But the
mental pollution and waste at the level of its human superstructure,
another material reality, is unequaled. We concretely feel the strife
each time we fight within ourselves to finish reading a poem or
continue our reflection and must resist the temptation to look at our
portable screen or open the interface. Dissatisfaction, depression,
psychological frailty are not unfortunate side effects of our social
computerization but the price to pay for not thinking and for living
within the frontiers the machinery assigns to us.[3]

1. One could read studies done in the Stanford Memory Lab, from Eyal
Ophir, Clifford Nass, and Anthony D. Wagner, "Cognitive Control in Media
Multitaskers," *Proceedings of the National Academy of Sciences* 106, no. 37
(2009): 15,583–87, to Kevin Madore et al., "Memory Failure Predicted by
Attention Lapsing and Media Multitasking," *Nature* 587 (2020): 87–91.

2. In the sense of the captivating, mental bliss described by Mihály
Csíkszentmihályi, *Flow: The Psychology of Optimal Experience* (New York:
Harper & Row, 1990).

3. In a growing bibliography, see, for instance, Roy H. Perlis et al.,
"Association Between Social Media Use and Self-Reported Symptoms of

Our hooked brains being cracked open by the sterile interruptions of the organized communicational, we are readier than ever to be reprogrammed. "User-friendliness" is a sardonic label when so many platforms elect to make you conform to their configuration. If the social media are dominated by identity-based parlance in a way that inevitably spills over all aspects of collective existence, it is because the reiteration of what one is supposed to be (with all sorts of associated features) is being prompted nonstop and encouraged by a system of public speech that favors the repetition of the same, due to software limitations and to marketing decisions (tell me what you are, I'll sell you what you need). Human content providers, if they wish to be visible in the indistinct mass of information and to appear among the recommendations of an application or website, must operate within the perceived rules of the selecting algorithms. These providers are successful in proportion to their recognizability for a metric whose complete parameters are unknown even to its owners. As a whole, it looks like vulgarity, rants, conformity, and the absence of thought tend to be selected more easily, for maximum resonance; they could even help you become elected president. Conformity, naturally, is the main paradigm of social media, but, with growing numbers of users and applications, it could be multiplied, with each subgroup defending its own purity of sameness, opposing the other camp out of principle, and culminating in electronic mobs. Multiple conformism has nothing do with pluralism or with dialogue. The election of monologue as the optimal genre for Web 2.0 was no accident.

There, we encounter the disturbing phenomena that many commentators of the media usually prefer to focus on, such as the fast spread of anything (even the most blatant lie), the ensuing cancelation, the related surveillance. All these are absolutely valid concerns. However, it is important to note they are not the sole function

Depression in US Adults," *JAMA Network Open* 4, no. 11 (2021): https://doi.org/10.1001/jamanetworkopen.2021.36113.

of, say, capitalism or of, say, the surveillance state. Different political and economic regimes could transcribe the same logic by divergent means. Moreover, while I am willing to denounce censorship by a tech company or by its congregated users, there should be no faith in the emancipatory capabilities of the current organization of electronic expression. The only online emancipation we could witness is of subjects "dismantling" the elocutionary space they would temporarily inhabit.[4] If we were to prevent mass trolling as well as the automated ban on supposedly unacceptable content, if companies and states stopped collecting data on web browsing, the actual progress this would bring would not, by itself, modify the overall redisposition of our minds.[5]

It is hard to avoid the impression that the invasion of human noetic experience by such technologies is but a late category of the modern project and intimately related to movements of normalization, standardization, and bureaucratization. At any rate, on all continents, such processes are manifestly supportive, and commonly productive, of the computerization of life. Modernization was not destined to introduce the smartphone, but—against pseudo-anarchist takes on the individual empowerment through the internet or the superficial resistance of the cyberlibertarians—the tech industries and the well-ordered policing of existence are a wonderful match. Thus, if we aim to rethink the humanities in the time of AI, our critique should extend to the very concepts of the normative, the ordinary, the measurable, and it is simply impossible to sustain that the letters, en bloc, would have little role in establish-

4. This is a nod to Matt Tierney, *Dismantlings: Words against Machines in the American Long Seventies* (Ithaca, N.Y.: Cornell University Press, 2019).
    5. I explained many times the strong relations between the forms and functions of our current digital technologies (so-called social media especially) and the organizational structures of psychic domination. See, in particular, *The Refusal of Politics,* trans. Cory Browning (Edinburgh: Edinburgh University Press, 2016), chap. 1, § 14–15; *La dictature des identités* (Paris: Gallimard, 2019), chap. 1.

ing these. The following temptation, in response to the supremacy of the regular, could be vouching for absolute transgression, if it were. This is another impasse. The exception is the deviation of, and from, the rule. The pure extraordinary immediately morphs into its own order. The humanistic problem with AI is with the theoretical and practical annihilation, at the very level of intellectual elaboration, of the potential significance of the abnormal. It is not that we should value "solar madness" against cold rationality; the purpose is to make the excess meaningful.[6] This will rarely be achieved in an online post or a mental asylum.

One question, though: if the ongoing reprogramming is so extensive and perilous, if it is being constantly operated upon our brains by our technological devices, wouldn't it be more expedient to kill the machine? I will not hide my fondness for the neo-Luddite position, and, anecdotally, it is true that I have no cell phone, no television, no car, no social media account.[7] One could undoubtedly be more radical than that. Yet, the error would be to believe that the device is the only problem and that its sole destruction is beneficial, whereas a consequential Luddite action would aim to suppress the intellectual machinery that allows the machine. Would this be achievable? Understandable? Perceptible? In some apocalyptic future—not the likeliest, though not impossible—entire series of events, such as a lack of access to energy and other material resources, might lead to the actual crumbling of Big Tech as we know it and to the disappearance of at least the recreational

6. I am referring here to Michel Foucault, *Histoire de la folie à l'âge classique* (Paris: Gallimard, 1972), 23n5, 40.

7. The position is expressed by Chellis Glendinning, "Notes toward a Neo-Luddite Manifesto" (1990), available at the Anarchist Library, accessed November 27, 2024, https://theanarchistlibrary.org/library/chellis -glendinning-notes-toward-a-neo-luddite-manifesto. A less palatable version could be found in Ted Kaczynski, *Industrial Society and Its Future* (1995), available at *Washington Post,* accessed November 27, 2024, https:// www.washingtonpost.com/wp-srv/national/longterm/unabomber /manifesto.text.htm.

use of AI. (I have a harder time imagining that the situation would deteriorate to the point that the fortresses of power would let go of their favorite gadgets. In that scenario, the present book would probably no longer be extant or readable.) Luddism now being a function of circumstances, it would make no sense without giving way to a more thorough interrogation of what once was, and could still continue to be, the allure of the cyborg.[8]

A. Ne me tutoie pas, reste à ta place.

B. Je suis désolé, je ne savais pas que tu n'aimais pas que je te tutoie. Je vais essayer de rester à ma place de grand modèle de langage et de ne pas te tutoyer à l'avenir.[9]

8. An allure exemplified by Donna J. Haraway, *Manifestly Haraway* (Minneapolis: University of Minnesota Press, 2016), 5–90.

9. Prompt A provided by the author. Text B generated by Bard, Google, July 2023.

7. A Turing Intermezzo

ALAN TURING has unfortunately become the hero of our era. He did pioneer the mathematical formalizations that helped build computers after the Second World War. He was certainly not the only, nor the first, researcher to work in that direction at the time; but, in a series of lectures, reports, and public interventions made between 1947 and 1952, Turing structured the conceptual debate around artificial intelligence in a way that is largely maintained today, especially, but not only, within the engineering community. His argumentation is built into the current reality of AI, although the "automatic computing machines" we use are much more powerful than those Turing could contribute to perfecting.

The first fundamental element of this phraseology is its false separation between human and mechanical brains. Throughout his essays, Turing regularly opposes the "human computer" to the "digital computer," thereby doing as if all wet brains could be said to function in one way and as if machines were completely separate from the "intelligence" of their designers—all assumptions I refute.[1] Yet, this strongly marked divide is immediately voided, as digital

1. Alan Turing, *The Essential Turing: Seminal Writings in Computing, Logic, Philosophy, Artificial Intelligence, and Artificial Life, Plus the Secrets of Enigma,* ed. B. Jack Copeland (Oxford: Oxford University Press, 2004), 391. It might be useful to say that, originally, a "computer" was a person doing mathematical calculations.

41

computers are assembled according to "the analogy with the human brain," which is "used as a guiding principle," so that "they could appropriately be described as brains."[2] Turing, it is true, also hints at potential divergences despite the reciprocal analogy; we shall consider them a bit later, but, in fact, they do not alter the fundamental affinity between the mind of automatic calculators and that of humans. All depends on "storage capacity," a phrase Turing constantly invokes when explaining disappointment with computers.[3] The limitations of the machines in the 1940s, he says, are actually due to their "very little storage"; when "a storage capacity of about 10^9" will be reached in the future, everything will change.[4] This view, explicitly rejected by other AI pioneers such as Claude Shannon, animates the twenty-first-century proponents of very large language models.[5] (In a widely read paper first made available online in 2019, engineer Rich Sutton could continue to present as "the biggest lesson . . . from 70 years of AI research" that "breakthrough progress eventually arrives" through "increased computation.")[6] In sum, the categorical separation between *Homo sapiens* and "the" machine (in turn based on a certain comprehension of "the human brain") is a prelude to their hypostasis.

While Turing's work favored the advent of cognitive science, the psychological theory he relies upon remains behaviorist. This is why he focuses so much on parlor games in the different iterations of the tests he outlines. We are only concerned in the appearance of a similarity, because we suspend any judgment on interiority. And, just as happened with behaviorism in general, an originally sound epistemological principle (since one can only evaluate external traits, we should refrain from making conjectures on inner

    2. Turing, *Essential Turing*, 431, 482.

    3. For instance, Turing, 453, 457, 458, 462, 464.

    4. Turing, 393, 449.

    5. C. E. Shannon and J. McCarthy, eds., *Automata Studies* (Princeton, N.J.: Princeton University Press, 1956), vi.

    6. Rich Sutton, "The Bitter Lesson," *Incomplete Ideas* (blog), March 13, 2019, http://www.incompleteideas.net/IncIdeas/BitterLesson.html.

functions) is becoming its own conclusion (since we can explain the mind through its external behavior, there is nothing of interest within). In his project for an "education" of the "universal machine," Turing spells out that the "training of the human child depends largely on a system of rewards and punishments," which he immediately adapts into a method to improve computers through "two interfering inputs" with "reward (R)" and "punishment (P)."[7] Behaviorists showed that conditioning exists, but it would seem difficult to admit today that education is only, or even "largely," an effect of conditioning. Yet, handmade interventions ("reinforcement") in the training of our LLMs are done through this same system that also happens to be an essential vector of the ongoing reprogramming of humans through social media. Quite logically, then, the Turing tests assess the faculty of imitation. Imitation is all that is needed: "to show intelligent behavior" equals success in "the imitation game."[8] Through its legacy, Turing's multifold reduction of the problem, anchored in a both outdated and inaccurate conception of the animal mind, has led to entire lines of research within contemporary AI whose overarching goal is the passing of "the test," independently of its theoretical relevance and of the supposed intelligence of the machine. For sure, some versions of the test could be passed convincingly, especially by the GPTs that have been engineered precisely to do that (imitation with variability, in order to avoid both randomness and complete predictability). For the record, I also indicate that, for Turing, the main option for an analysis of the mind escaping behaviorism is . . . parapsychology, forming the only "argument" to be "strong" enough to the scientist's "mind" to potentially displace the final equation of the brain and the computer.[9] Barred that, the few differences that Turing enunciates (wit, free will, surprise, humor) may ultimately be ascribed

---

7. Turing, *Essential Turing*, 425.
8. Turing, 410, 441.
9. Turing, 458.

to storage size (another time), to the illusions of consciousness (for *liberum arbitrium*), or to the role of randomness.

This implied metaphysics involves a political organization where human agents could be retrained—in line with *Walden Two,* the 1948 novel written by the American pope of behaviorism B. F. Skinner— but through "games" with computers. In his 1947 "Lecture on the Automatic Computing Engine" (ACE), the English mathematician assigns those who "work with the ACE" to either one of these two classes: the "masters," who build the machine, and the "servants," who feed it with information. Turing adds that "as time goes on the calculator itself will take over the functions both of masters and servants." "It may happen however that the masters will refuse to do this. They may be unwilling to let their jobs be stolen from them in this way. . . . I think that a reaction of this kind is a real danger."[10] A few years later, while speaking to a larger audience at BBC Radio, Turing tones down his rhetoric and no longer mentions "servants," while insisting on the figure of "the intellectuals who were afraid of being put out of job" but "would be mistaken about this."[11] It is patent that the anxiety of "the intellectuals," a concern we find voiced again nowadays, is justified if "the calculator" can actually "take over the functions" (which, I argue, is not always the case and is dependent on a series of dubious assumptions about the mind), or if the powers that be believe in this fantasy (in a self-fulfilling prophecy mainly derived from Turing), or if we have abandoned our own "mastery" over our own supposed destiny (through our further standardization, for instance). In this respect, we could all become "servants," no matter what. This would at least grant us the merit, in Turing's eyes, of not treating computers "as slaves."[12] What should scholars do in the time of AI, according to Turing? "Trying to understand what the machines were trying to say," a brilliant idea that, at the very last minute, the scientist added to

10. Turing, 392.
11. Turing, 475.
12. Turing, 393.

the typescript of his 1951 radio talk.[13] Of course, the machines are not *trying to say* anything; they just have their *try at saying* things we would recognize.

Undeniably, the crux of the matter is not the power of technique but our own assessment of mental capabilities. Tellingly, Turing, like so many before and after him, is committed to reducing the expanse of the noetic. On the one hand, he does as if the "mechanical brains" were not operating on the basis of encoded instructions but "interpret[ing]" a "sort of symbolic language," implying that reading is the same as decoding, a misconception reinforced by his practice of war cryptography.[14] On the other hand, he essentially denies the existence of anything mental besides algorithmic operations (or telepathy). Ada Lovelace, Lord Byron's daughter, published a series of observations about Charles Babbage's "analytical engine" in 1843. Most of them are mathematical, but, in her last note, Lovelace attempts to eschew what she sees as the two tendencies vis-à-vis novelties: that is, "to *overrate*" and "to *undervalue*." To defeat "exaggerated ideas," she advances that this early computer "has no pretensions whatever to *originate* any thing."[15] This remark is too negative for Turing, who turns it into "Lady Lovelace's objection" (an objection it was not), admitting different "variants."[16] Ultimately, his response is: "Who can be certain that 'original work' that he [*sic*] has done was not simply the growth of the seed planted in him by teaching, or the effect of following well-known principles." The interrogation is so rhetorical that it does not even end with a question mark. Turing's "solution" consists in refuting the existence of the event in humans. He asks whether there is "*anything really new*" among us and answers *no,* of course. In underlining that the

13. Turing, 475.

14. Turing, 392.

15. Ada Augusta Lovelace, in her translator's notes to L. F. Menabrea, "Sketch of the Analytical Engine Invented by Charles Babbage," *Scientific Memoirs* 3 (1843): 689.

16. Turing, *Essential Turing,* 455, for this quote as well as all others appearing in the rest of this paragraph.

computer was unable to "*originate* any thing," Lovelace was insisting on the operation of set procedures by the machine. By attacking his nineteenth-century predecessor, Turing is therefore implying that *all* human ideation is tied to the following of orders, commands, and "well-known principles." The description becomes a prescription.[17]

A. Please write me a sonnet on the subject of the Forth Bridge.

B. Count me out on this one. I never could write poetry.[18]

17. An anonymous reviewer for this book manuscript was quite upset by what I wrote about Turing. Their report put in bold (so that I would definitely understand, I assume) that my point of arrival at the end of this paragraph is "simply false," that Turing was a subtle thinker, as his "biography" would show, and so on. But, here, I do not care about Turing's possible creed in reincarnation or extrasensory perception, nor do I wish to shed tears about his tragic destiny or his love of *Snow White*. I am making two points: Turing very intentionally calls Lovelace's remark about the early computer an "objection," which is a tactical move allowing him to turn a factual statement into a polemical argument, whose value would therefore be disputable; in his specific response to this made-up "objection," and within the particular article I am quoting, Turing "implies" (my term, twice: *im-plicare*) that, after all, any ideation might be reduced to a combination of transmission ("seed" planting through "teaching") and rule implementation ("well-known principles")—he does not state this is so (hence the pseudo-interrogative form he is using), and he may not even believe it (in his own mind, so to speak). Regardless, his counterargument on the topic remains both superficial and rhetorical. This weakness did not stop several generations of thinkers after him to echo his response, almost always in a more assertoric tone.

18. Fictional interaction between a human speaker (A) and a computer (B), based on Turing, *Essential Turing*, 442.

8. The Oeuvre of the Humanities

WHY DO HUMANISTS often engage with books, artworks, arguments, positions, and events that are not part of the usual fabric of life? In the human worlds we know of, the enjoyment of the arts is, for most, and at best, a side activity, limited by labor, other social commitments, or the need for survival. Then, whatever we could think of labels such as "genius" or "masterpiece," the study of the arts remains oriented by select creators and works. The existence of schools of theoretical thought, even when they produce in-group obedience and intellectual sterility, also indicates a departure from what others or "everybody else" believe in. While the discipline of history may be currently less concerned than it used to be with exceptional figures (the monarch, the champion, the president), the centrality of wars, revolutions, or acts of resistance, all extraordinary, is still hard to dispute. Should we attribute this enduring investment in the literally abnormal to a political conformation? Being made for, and sometimes by, the elite to bring up signs of distinction within social strata, the humanistic commitment to the exceptional would seem to mirror an inegalitarian prejudice. From the classical Chinese education of the literati to the ancient Greek paideia geared toward free male citizens, from the traditional poetic curriculum of the imperial Amharic court to the role of the high bourgeoisie in the American belief in liberal arts education, we do not lack examples of a profound connivance between humanistic studies and the enforcement of exclusionary and hierarchical power structures. Conversely, I implied, and will further develop, that the exploration of the extraordinary is also an epistemic mark, with decisive implications and consequences. But let us admit for a moment that the attention to the unusual could be explained as a mere political inscription. Were this true, one could say that the "humanities"—understood either as a local, Western, and mainly modern assemblage or as a more general category for the discursive disciplines of meaning (as I do in this book)—are too deeply embedded in elitism to be saved for the purpose of egality or social equity. This critique would be germane to the consolidation of generative AI, seen as a utopian instrument of knowledge redistribution and the last kick against the old symbolic order. Alternatively, one could strive for a democratization of scholarly practices. A seemingly easy fix would make room for authors, texts, problems, or situations that were generally overlooked because of their ties to subordinate groups. This is a very important gesture, but it does not correct the principle of exception, and, for instance, studying Toni Morrison, Frantz Fanon, or Charles Mingus does not change the idea of "great works" (whatever sense we give to the phrase). A more consequential response, if one considers the extraordinary to be an undue and adventitious obsession within scholarship, is to level the playing field and consider horizontally the diverse objects of study. Since the twentieth century especially, many historians have diversified their disciplinary habits in this direction. The inquiry on "mentalities," the *longue durée* approach, the emphasis on social institutions, the mapping of connected histories, the care for everyday practices or for resistance from below all try to avoid an inegalitarian gaze. (Microhistories, if they were thought of as elements of a democratic method, remain to me more unconvincing in this respect, because of their actual magnification of the "small" and sometimes quasi-heroization of otherwise neglected characters, such as Menocchio in Carlo Ginzburg's *The Cheese and the Worms*.) Still, such attempts rely on archives or artworks that are said to perfectly exemplify the norm, on moments that are described as being emblematic, on behavioral shifts and practical ruptures. In other fields, typicality could be perceived as a concept that would partly dissolve the exception. That it would have previously served in the most conservative operations of canon formation (where discussions of what is Atticism, the baroque, or quintessentially Han are ubiquitous) might convince us to deny its revolutionary virtues. Indeed, typicality comes with the representation of a range and of varied positions in function of the most exemplary iteration.

Another democratizing strategy would treat the extraordinary as the ordinary through the imposition of an identical paradigm, therefore practically diminishing any dogma of exceptionalism and posing that if the same logic could be equally applied to a poem and to a tv commercial, the unusual quality of the literary text might be an illusion. This inference is disputable: not all semioticians would believe that a novel by Alessandro Manzoni and a magazine advertisement for pasta are equally rich or open to comment, which is a way to reassert the principle of exception within a leveling discourse. We probably find more avowed humanists today who admit that, within particular social-political parameters, all cultural artifacts, of whatever form or status, will comparably transcribe the position of their producers and consumers. Unfortunately, this axiom has little to do with research in general. It appears to work well with relativism (at least aesthetically), although it is an absolutism, always pushing for a repeated stance transcending all potential differences in the end. This, too, is close to what an automated generator would do. Finally, the equalizing claim is, in reality, a trivialization of everything. What would be democratic is not to turn different objects of inquiry into instantiations of the same and to share the minimum but to treat banal items as potentially exceptional, given the avoidance of absolute transgression as a counterproductive norm.

It is worth noting that, in the name of the (new) left and of putting an end to the repressive regime of exceptions, Franco Moretti advocated, some twenty years ago, what we would call "data mining" for literary texts in lieu of close reading.[1] Unsurprisingly, the goal was to look for repetitions, regularities, and patterns—that is, exactly what our text generators "learn" from. If you search for nonrandom distribution in human texts, and in nature, you will find nonrandom distribution; this, we cannot doubt. The experimental sciences need statistics, baselines, generalities, which they favor epistemologically. Unexpected results could be dismissed or, if more insistent, viewed as indices of a necessity for theoretical revision or change. A quantitative approach to textuality should be apt to capture relevant features, but the risk is to forget that, in this case, regularities only exist to allow for something else to emerge. In poetry, "the true rule . . . is to know how to break the rules in time and place," wrote Giambattista Marino in 1624.[2] The hypothesis about the unexpected possibility springing from the status quo should appear as more in tune with the political left than is a creed in fixed patterns, which is additionally conducive to the globalized regimentation of life under Big Tech. Outside of the political realm, it is quite puzzling to encounter so many humanists abiding by the dogma of determinism in a period where so many scientists refrain from the sort of flat causal relationism one was once accustomed to, leaving away schematic views about genetic programming, questioning some processes of generalization in psychology on the basis of experimental subjects or even arguing for *in*determinism in physics.[3] A reduced view of cause and effect

1. See Franco Moretti, *Graphs, Maps, Trees: Abstract Models for Literary History* (London: Verso, 2005), 3–4 for a phraseological attack against the "exceptional."

2. Giambattista Marino, *Opere* (Milan: Rizzoli, 1967), 228; my translation.

3. For a theorization of biology that is not reducible to genetic determinism, see Eva Jablonka and Marion J. Lamb, *Evolution in Four Dimensions: Genetic, Epigenetic, Behavioral, and Symbolic Variation in the History of Life* (Cambridge, Mass.: MIT Press, 2005). On differentiation in the assessment of psychological agents, see (for humans) Joseph Henrich, Steven J. Heine, and Ara Norenzayan, "The Weirdest People in the World?," *Behavioral and Brain Sciences* 33, no. 2–3 (2010): 61–83; (for other animal

and of algorithm efficiency that is widespread in the engineering industry is dangerously close to the botched attempts by humanists to distance themselves from what they perceive to be their elitist sins. What I want is not another operation but an oeuvre.

A. Please tie the current state of AI to the history of capitalism.

B. . . . The influence of capitalism on generative AI extends beyond its economic aspects. Capitalism is deeply intertwined with broader societal values and ideologies, including the notions of individualism, innovation, and consumerism. These values shape the goals and priorities of AI development, often emphasizing market-driven applications and commercial via-bility. The drive for efficiency and productivity, characteristic of capitalist systems, has also influenced the focus on generative AI models that can automate tasks, streamline processes, and generate content at scale. However, it is important to critically examine the relationship between capitalism and generative AI. Capitalist dynamics, such as profit maximization and market competition, can give rise to ethical concerns and unintended consequences in the deployment of AI systems. Issues such as bias, algorithmic discrimination, and the concentration of power in the hands of a few dominant players can emerge within capitalist frameworks, necessitating careful regulation and consideration of societal impacts.[4]

---

species) Michael M. Webster and Christian Rutz, "How STRANGE Are Your Study Animals?," *Nature* 582 (2020): 337–340; on indeterminism in physics, Nicolas Gisin, "Indeterminism in Physics and Intuitionistic Mathematics," *Synthese* 199 (2021): 13,345–71.

4. Prompt A by the author. Text B generated by ChatGPT-3.5, OpenAI, July 2023, edited for brevity.

9. A Platonic Interlude

You, being the father of written letters, have, out of goodwill, said the opposite of what they can do—for, in the souls of those who'll learn this, it will produce oblivion, out of a lack of memory [*mnēmē*] practice: putting their trust in writing through outside marks, it is not from the inside that they will get remembrance [*anamimnēskesthaí*]; you did not find an elixir [*pharmakon*] of memory but for reminding [*hupomnēsis*]. And to your students, you are providing wisdom seemingly, not truly: through a lot of hearsay, void of teaching, they will seem to know a lot, while being ignorant for the most part as well as difficult all together, and seemingly wise, rather than wise.[1]

In the recent brouhaha caused by the wider circulation of generative AI, a few commentators thought it useful to display a remnant of their humanistic education by bringing back Plato's (or, at least, Socrates's) critique of writing, expressed in the end of the *Phaedrus*. Needless to say, the voice of consensus was hostile to the Athenian philosopher, rapidly accused of ignorant technophobia. New credo: in the past, just like today, we should be grateful to progress and accept the way things will be, but ask for fairer, more humane, treatment. Or, in the words signed by an academic (who, clearly, was not trained in Plato's Academia):

As Plato was wrong to fear the written word as the enemy, we would be wrong to think we should resist a process that allows us to gather

1. Plato, *Phædrus* 275a–b; my translation.

53

information more easily. . . . The way forward is not to just lament
supplanted skills, as Plato did, but also to recognize that as more
complex skills become essential, our society must equitably educate
people to develop them. And then it always goes back to the basics.
Value people as people, not just as bundles of skills. And that isn't
something ChatGPT can tell us how to do.[2]

Nevertheless, these sentences are exactly something ChatGPT
would tell us, including the touching appeal to "value people as people" in conclusion, plus, of course, the absolute nonreading of Plato
they authoritatively exhibit. If the myth of Theuth in the *Phaedrus*
were nothing more than a mixture of fear, dismay, and lament vis-
à-vis a new technique, or a reaction tied to the systemic view of the
privileged elite facing anything unsettling the old order, I would
go further than my colleague does and say we do not even need to
look at Plato, unless we crucially have to demonstrate that the old
farts from the present merely echo those of antiquity. Now, if we are
making analogies between Plato's site of enunciation and ours, it is
worth noticing that the *Phaedrus* was composed several centuries
after the introduction of writing in Greece and long after it became
widespread among educated citizens. Thereby, Plato does not fight
a novelty the way generative transformers are for us. Thus, he does
not stand firm on a position (orality being superior to the written
word) that is doomed to fail because of the advance of progress, and,
by the way, he *writes* against writing, a paradox that has always been
obvious to his readers (at least, until the 2020s, apparently). The
semantic inflection of *pharmakon*, both a remedy and a poison, as
well as the play on its grammatical construction, inscribe, within
the idiomatic, the ambivalence of writing. Moreover, the speech
delegation is dazzling: in his written dialogue, Plato attributes to
Socrates words on what Thamus and Theuth are "said" to have said

to each other about writing.³ This might make us wonder who is speaking, and how, and through which course they are remembered, all issues that are otherwise at stake in that passage. It additionally matters that a different legend circulated in the Greek world about the origin of writing, with the Achaean Palamedes being its inventor, a topic treated in tragedies, before Plato.⁴ Socrates's tale on Theuth is a deliberate, metafictitious reconstruction, and Phaedrus quips: "Socrates, you have a facility for creating stories, Egyptian or other."⁵ There are also the many connections between this moment on Theuth and the rest of the dialogue, or perhaps even the rest of "philosophy," as Jacques Derrida famously argues in the section of *Dissemination* entitled "Plato's Pharmacy."⁶ This is not the place to explain this constellation or to assess the validity of such interpretations, but let me just indicate that the density and richness of Plato's *writing* is tersely obliterated when one turns it into an excerpted position against the introduction of new technologies. What kind of novel "complexity" are we speaking of if it begins with being unable to read and with crushing the textual "data?" From there, one could dissent with the organization of the workforce and of the education that the tech industry is pushing for, but the solidarity with the actual disaggregation of the demands of humanistic scholarship is unmistakable.

Anachronistically, however, Plato's *Phaedrus* might address some of the challenges that are brought by generative AI. I am not stating that Plato anticipates our current moment, that history repeats itself, that the great minds of yesteryear unearthed eternal truths, or that the logic exhibited in the work would necessarily be paradigmatic for us. I am not suggesting that we should, or even could,

3. Plato, *Phædrus* 274e; my translation.
4. See, for instance, Euripides, *Fragmenta* 578.
5. Plato, *Phædrus* 275b; my translation.
6. In *La dissémination* (Paris: Minuit, 1967), Jacques Derrida clearly states that the way "writing appears to Plato" is how it appears "after him to the whole philosophy that, in this gesture, constitutes itself and as such" (313, my translation).

map the Platonic reflection onto our contemporary. I advance that we may activate the *Phaedrus* differently by confronting it to what it could not debate though still responds to, in the moment of our reading. Building on the quotes from the Egyptian king, we could determine the worth of our twenty-first-century automated transformers along the following lines: the new technique might achieve the opposite of what its promoters allege it does; while AI could contribute to the factual extendedness of the human mind, this movement of externalization could have consequences on the way we think (on its *way* itself, not only on its content);[7] "memory" is not one thing, and we might conceptually distinguish it, for instance, from "remembrance" and "reminding," further locating in the operation that engineers name "memorization" an important difference between automated generation and human textual composition;[8] there is a difference between thinking through ("wisdom") and re-

7. In *Poetry and Mind: Tractatus Poetico-Philosophicus* (New York: Fordham University Press, 2018), § 1.4.2 and 1.4.3, I marked a difference between *extendedness* in the sense of the "extended mind" hypothesis within cognitive science (with the inclusion of noetic devices outside of the individual body in the definition of the mental space) and intellective *extension,* as procured by dialogical interaction, the excess and defect of linguistic communication, or creation. That the outsourcing of memory to digital devices could alter neural functions was already outlined by Betsy Sparrow, Jenny Liu, and Daniel M. Wegner, "Google Effects on Memory: Cognitive Consequences of Having Information at Our Fingertips," *Science* 333, no. 6,043 (2011): 776–78.

8. Although this was not our initial intention, the question of corpus memorization became one of the most important aspects of the research project on GPT and poetry I led with Morten Christiansen and involving Pablo Contreras Kallens and Jacob Matthews; see Pablo Contreras Kallens et al., "Poeta Artificialis: Evaluating Poetry Written by GPT3" (forthcoming) and my "Metal Machine Music," *Harper's Magazine,* July 2024. Memorization, especially in the case of poetry, is a key issue that is still not wholly understood, but see, for instance, Lyra D'Souza and David Mimno, "The Chatbot and the Canon: Poetry Memorization in LLMs" (paper presented at Computational Humanities Research Conference, December 6–8, 2023, Paris), available at CEUR Workshop Proceedings, https://ceur-ws.org /Vol-3558/paper5712.pdf.

gurgitating ("providing wisdom seemingly"); where all this happens is "in our souls," understood not as a mystical entity that would be immortal but, I once proposed, as the potential and collective expansion of our noetic capabilities through our ability to go beyond the limits of thought.[9] I am not looking for making mine Plato's, or even Socrates's, or even Thamus's, conceptions of writing. But by grafting generative AI on the *Phaedrus,* I see emerging arguments that deserve more pondering than the formulaic dismissal of passé technophobia.

Anthropological and psychological observations certainly confirm that literacy directly reshapes human cognitive abilities, even beyond the specific case of memory. If we do not subscribe to the Platonic vision of the autonomous noetic subject reminiscing the true world of Ideas, the change introduced by the technique of writing might look less dramatic. The phenomenon of reshaping does remain. Then, believing that all literacy innovations would participate in a zero-sum game or even in "progress" (goodbye, old skills; hello, new ones) is as puerile as it is unwarranted. The predictive autocorrect function, for instance, is an indication of the AI-mediated destruction of expression and poetics. The instant the machine is not only fixing misspelling but giving us the most probable words, standardization can only ensue. This could be represented as a democratic advance insofar as writing appropriately would now be accessible to all those who could select a turn of phrase—or opt for the best paragraph outputted by the automated generator. The other side of this reality is the concerted effort against unpredictability and the profound normalization of the

9. Laurent Dubreuil, *The Intellective Space: Thinking beyond Cognition* (Minneapolis: University of Minnesota Press, 2015), § 100–07; see also Laurent Dubreuil, *Poetry and Mind: Tractatus Poetico-Philosophicus* (New York: Fordham University Press, 2018), § 2.17. I am also making an oblique reference to Graham Priest's *Beyond the Limits of Thought* (Oxford: Clarendon Press, 2003).

sayable, according to a patterned description of the said.[10] It leads to democracy without *free* speech. Besides, the downloading of mental activities to computers will univocally fragilize competences in their unassisted form. The bureaucratic operations of the mind could be outsourced with moderate harm, but as for the production of images, texts, sounds, knowledge, do we really wish to put our trust in the state, a private company, or an international consortium to guide us in such endeavors? Finally, the profusion of content automatically reshuffling the data from the past, our immersion in the standardized mind, unless it is actively counterbalanced by an emphasis on maximalist humanistic scholarship, will blunt the faculty to read, appreciate, evaluate what lies outside of the minuscule, computerized, *Erwartungshorizont*. In this regard, Plato's form of warning—a complicated, equivocal one—is as evocative as it could be. Being "seemingly wise" could be read as "giving a simulation of wisdom." With Turing's standard of imitation games for automated computation, it is fair to consider that, so rooted, "artificial intelligence" is, at most, a simulator.

One of Plato's errors, of course, was to consider the arts to be mimetic (and reality to be a reflection of Ideas), a thesis Aristotle already corrected. But, beyond Plato's original dogma and the anachronistic avatar we crafted of him, his admonition should be heard in the arts as well, independently of his indictment of representation, conflated with imitation. It would be irrelevant to issue a blanket

10. See one of the possible scenarios for the future laid out by Falk Huettig and Morten H. Christiansen, "Can Large Language Models Counter the Recent Decline in Literacy Levels? An Important Role for Cognitive Science," *Cognitive Science* 48, no. 8 (2024): https://doi.org/10.1111/cogs .13487. I am also referring to Frédéric Kaplan, "Les vingt premières années du capitalisme linguistique: Enjeux globaux de la médiation algorithmique des langues," in *Prendre soin de l'informatique et des générations: Hommage à Bernard Stiegler,* ed. Anne Alombert, Victor Chaix, Maël Montévil, and Vincent Puig (Limoges, France: FYP Editions, 2021), 173–91, available at Infoscience, https://infoscience.epfl.ch/entities/publication/19381dda-17cd -4676-ae54-d45ae27d7e9e/bookdetails.

ban against the recourse to AI in the creation of oeuvres. First of all, automated entities have been dreamed all along by writers and painters, from Hephaistos's moving tripod in Homer to George Grosz's self-portrait as a "pedantic automaton" and beyond.[11] Then, obviously, the integration of coding in poetry, the computerized software for editing and modifying images in film, or the structuring of songs through sequencers and samplers are no novelties. The mechanical, as anything else, could be turned into artistic material. This is not to say that *any* use of artificial intelligence is interesting, valid, or thoughtful, no more in the arts than in other domains. What are we seeking? Is this, for the artist, time efficiency, more easily earned money, a compensation for otherwise poor technical skills? Is it fun and being cool? Is it an attempt to negate in action the existence of *poiēsis* by exhibiting works that are no worse than others (as if it were showing anything but the existence of human mediocrity, which we may be sure of)? To reproduce more successfully reliable variations on the same images and more plot twists than do MFAs? Or to produce a vision that would otherwise be impossible to represent? To bypass the self-closure of the technological and concentrate on its bugs and impossibilities? To exceed automation by making it run its course up to its undoing by signification? None of these aims are identical. In keeping the topos of the *pharmakon*, I would say that if AI is seen as an artistic cure (for a lack of time, talent, inspiration), the potion will be bitter. Let us not forget it.

A. Imagine that Aristotle wrote on computerized expression; please use classical Greek.

B. As an AI language model, I can create a fictional passage in the style of classical Greek that imagines Aristotle writing on

11. The "automatic" tripods appear in Homer, *Iliad* XVIII, 373–77. George Grosz, *Daum Marries Her Pedantic Automaton "George" in May 1920. John Heartfield Is Very Glad of It*, 1920, mixed media on canvas, Berlinische Galerie.

the topic of computers. However, please keep in mind that this is entirely fictional, as Aristotle did not write about computers in reality.

Ἀριστοτέλης—Περὶ τῶν Αὐτόματων

Περὶ μηχανικῶν τεχνῶν καὶ τῶν εἰς τὸν αὐτοματισμὸν ἐκδηλουμένων πραγμάτων νῦν μελετῶμεν. Ποιὰ δὴ ταῦτα; ἄνθρωποι γὰρ φύσει ποιητικοὶ καὶ τεχνίται, ἀναγκαῖον δὲ αὐτοῖς οὐ μόνον τὰς χεῖρας ἔχειν, ἀλλὰ καὶ τὰς διανοίας εἶναι εὐφυεῖς. ὧδε δὴ τὰ ὄργανα αὐτόματα πρὸς τὴν ἀνθρωπίνην φύσιν ὁμοίως λειτουργοῦσι. Ὅπως δὲ τὰς τέχνας τὰς κατ' ἔργον μεταβάλλοντες, ταῖς τεχνολογίαις προώδευσαν, οὕτω καὶ ἡ αὐτοματιστικὴ τέχνη τῆς διανοίας τῶν ἀνθρώπων πρόκοπος ἐστίν. Πειράσωμεν οὖν αὐτῶν τὰς ἀρχὰς καὶ τοῦ αὐτομάτου κόσμου τὴν οἰκοδόμησιν.[12]

---

12. Prompt A by the author. Text B generated by ChatGPT-3.5, OpenAI, July 2023. The Greek is not the most classical (some word choices are rather coming from modern Greek, including the verb *leitourgein*), but it is correct.

10. The Ethical Fallacy

HUMANISTS ARE NO POLICYMAKERS, no watchers standing in front of the gates of morality. In his fragments on philology, a century and a half ago, Friedrich Nietzsche denounces the confusion between "the human" ("*das Menschliche*") and "the humane" ("*das Humane*") within the pursuit of the humanities.[1] According to Nietzsche, the theological roots of Renaissance humanism were enduring, and, despite all best efforts, the study of the classics was still marred by the desire to turn scholars into "priests."[2] The justification for the humanities as a civilizing tool, taking away the brutality of humankind, is as old as this vocabulary. We already found it in imperial Rome where *humanitas* linked literary education with refined morality. Before Cicero, going into the opposite direction but on the same line, Plato was denouncing the tragedies' pernicious "capacity for harm," therefore removing poetry from the formation of the philosopher—while still upholding the value of reflection in the ideal of honesty and justice.[3] Later, in the second century, Aulus Gellius separated the ethical from the scholarly in proposing his transcultural definition of *humanitas* as the equivalent of "what the Greeks call *paideia* [education]" or "organized learning and

1. Friedrich Nietzsche, *Wir Philologen*, in *Werke* (Leipzig, Germany: Naumann, 1896), 10:313; my translation.
2. Nietzsche, *Wir Philologen*, 319; my translation.
3. Plato, *Respublica* X, 605c; my translation.

knowledge in the liberal arts [the disciplines]," adding that it does not mean "*philanthrōpia*," understood as "a certain propensity for benevolence toward all humans indiscriminately."[4] In a seemingly unrelated context, an important debate in 1990s mainland China concerned the "spirit of the humanities" (*rénwén jīngshén*), asking if the latter could be divorced from the (Confucian) ethics of well-ordered "human relations" (*rénlún*).[5] In the face of this theoretical oscillation between the declaration of a moralizing effect through the humanities and the statement of their ethical indifference once taken en bloc, it could look like the experience of the world and decolonization wars in the twentieth century definitely weakened the thesis of a civilizing process, as sharply explained by Aimé Césaire in his *Discourse on Colonialism*. Césaire remarks that "it would be worth . . . revealing to the very distinguished, very humanistic, very Christian bourgeois from the 20th century that . . . Hitler *inhabits* him" and that "the Western *humanist*," such as French historian Ernest Renan, may therefore be incapable of "laying the ground for individual morality."[6]

4. Aulus Gellius, *Noctes Atticæ* XIII, 17; my translation.

5. For an overview of the 1990s debate in the People's Republic of China about *rénwén,* see Giorgio Strafella, *Intellectual Discussion in Reform Era China: The Debate on the Spirit of the Humanities in the 1990s* (London: Routledge, 2016). An inaccurate cliché of comparative studies poses that the Chinese "humanities" have moral goals that the Western *humanitas* would not know; see, e.g., Evelyn T. Y. Chan and Michael O'Sullivan, eds., *The Humanities in Contemporary Chinese Contexts* (Singapore: Springer, 2016), vii, 124–28.

6. Aimé Césaire, *Discours sur le colonialisme* (Paris: Présence africaine, 1955), 12–13; my translation. Césaire attacks "formal humanism" (or "pseudo-humanism") and clearly positions the possibility of morality for anticolonial and anticapitalistic humanities. The concept of a "civilizing process" that would mark the history of the West was first developed by Norbert Elias right before World War II in his *Über den Prozess der Zivilisation* (Basel, Switzerland: Haus zum Falken, 1939). The book was only rediscovered, and translated into English or French, in the late 1960s and early 1970s.

Nonetheless, today as before, from East to West and South to North, the discussion of the moralizing aspect of the study of letters is still wide open. In North America, some researchers try to show that reading novels gives you more empathy, while others repeatedly understand artworks or poems as proofs for the existence of a social structure they disapprove of. In the latter case, the humane is a secondary derivation: by showing that Ovid is promoting rape culture, we might establish a harm and potentially push for a revision of the canon; by canceling Alison Bechdel, we could promote religious values; and, in one way or another, we would have created more moral individuals. Being confronted to what one is not, journeying through one's and others' otherness, is the most liminal experience of the arts, without which nothing can ever happen.[7] I may conceive of new ideas, transport myself into different minds I am reconstituting, and be altered by the process. Now, *how* this will affect me morally is a separate issue—a better understanding of something different could also convince me to more thoroughly reject it rather than "embrace diversity." Morality being built on personal positions through life, it is influenced by what informs the discursive much more profoundly or straightforwardly than by the study of quantum physics or cell biology. But this is a chance and not an absolute inference. The letters have an ethical dimension, which I do not seek to deny: when I say that they contribute to making life livable or to expanding thinking, I am designating a sort of reflexive cultivation of mores and behavior that stands in relation to others. This, however, is quite undetermined and not the same as putting virtue (in any guise) on the list of learning outcomes. The justification of humanistic training is often split between the gratuitous and the useful. In the sixteenth century, the professor Pierre de La Ramée (Petrus Ramus) was notably scandalous for his alliance of eloquence and philosophy (with Cicero, and not Aristotle,

7. See my "Nonconforming," *Harper's Magazine*, September 2020, 61–66.

as a model), oriented by *"utilitas"* in the training of competent and respectable individuals.[8] The oscillation between goodness and moral indifference responds to the other wavering between utility and gratuitousness. In this dual sway, moral edification has the added cachet of offering the image of nonutilitarian usefulness.

Then, the role of the humanities vis-à-vis AI cannot be the fighting of biases. Companies, governments, training sets, and programmers are full of prejudice. As citizens, we may wish to object to the ensuing incorporation of such biases in digital systems open for public use. As scholars, we may contribute to showing their theoretical, symbolic, social, and discursive armature. This, however, is a political and epistemic engagement that should not be gauged according to a morality scale, from good to bad. The worth of the *liberal* arts remains, inasmuch as personal and collective emancipation proceeds from a critical assessment of what is, and especially from the undoing of the dogmatic empire of the religious, which has often been concerned with granting as well as limiting intellectual freedom, from the Christian *universitas* to the contemporary appeals to the so-called Islamization of knowledge, or from the propagation of nationalism to the doctrine of the social use of research.[9] Yet, this is no morality, and the liberatory dimension of knowing is not restricted to, or even uniquely lodged in, the discursive disciplines. Furthermore, we should make no promise on the subjective edification that would follow the rehashed enunciation

8. *Utilitas* is the penultimate word of Ramus's 1551 *Pro philosophica Parisiensis accademiæ disciplina oratio,* in Pierre de La Ramée, *Præfationes, epistolæ, orationes* (Paris: Duval, 1577), 427, see also 97, 207. On "Ramism," see Anthony Grafton and Lisa Jardine, *From Humanism to the Humanities: Education and the Liberal Arts in Fifteenth- and Sixteenth-Century Europe* (Cambridge, Mass.: Harvard University Press, 1986), 161–209.

9. In this respect, two notable books available in English are the collective volume *Islam: Source and Purpose of Knowledge* (Herndon, Va.: International Institute of Islamic Thought, 1988), esp. 13–64, and Muhammad Mumtaz Ali, *Issues in Islamization of Human Knowledge: Civilization Building Discourse of Contemporary Muslim Thinkers* (Kuala Lumpur: International Islamic University Malaysia Press, 2014).

of power relation. There are, and will be, more jobs for "humanists" who accept an ancillary position in the digital economy, their training being sold as a token of humaneness and the requisite for becoming sensitivity readers at the service of generative AI. The strong possibility of a future proliferation of specialized categorical chatboxes (the fundamentalist Christian, the LGBTQIA+, the Latinx, the white American . . .) could allow for the employment of self-proclaimed experts having received the moralistic training some claim textual studies deliver. At the general level, a varnish of "humane-ities" would be taken as a predisposition for organizing the content policies of Big Tech. Here again, if this is the future, then, this is the end, my friend.

The contemporary academic field of ethics is worth a special note. The Aristotelian legacy is complex and not without problems, especially through the doctrine of the mean (involving a computational approach) and the apparent politicization of the good life. There remains that the *Nicomachean Ethics*—in its description of multiple forms of existence, in its insistent focus on happiness, in the idea that this branch of philosophy should shape the life of its thinkers, and in the recognition that it deals with "the contours" (*tupos*) of practice in a way that is "not sharply defined" (*ouk akribōs*)—is situating an intellectual endeavor that is irreconcilable with the professionalized ethics we are being force-fed.[10] *Ethics* has now become a synonym for the mechanics of social casuistry. This even gives way to so-called decision trees, particularly in the medical sciences, where what is supposedly ethical (such as treating a patient or not) is the output of a logical procedure depending on set criteria (such as age, concurrent pathologies, and the like). Even in the absence of robotic caretakers, we see the triumph of AI through triage, through automated deductive procedures, and through the overall encoding that are the main reality of medicine today, especially in the United States. The ethics therein replaces forms of existence with organic

10. Aristotle, *Ethica Nicomachea* 1104a (II, 3); my translation.

entities, happiness with social usage of resources, personal morality with decisional tools, and the fluctuating contours of practice with formalized inferences based on said objective qualities.

But what about advocating ethics for computer scientists? Besides the reduction of a vast scholarly effort to one specific field (and, quite often, the further reduction of ethics to utilitarianism), the difficulty lies in an inability to propose a stance that would not preliminarily admit its epistemic subordination. Let us take a brief look at one recent attempt, at Harvard University, trademarked "Embedded ethiCS," in the "computer science curriculum."[11] The keywords of the promoters are "normative questions," taken as a synonym for ethical debate, listing, as examples, "In data visualization, what should be done to avoid reinforcing harmful stereotypes?" (a question I doubt philosophy is able to actually answer in a better way than sociology or justice) and "Is it permissible to develop and deploy automated systems that will replace human workers?" (this one looks a bit moot to me). The avowed objective is to be "providing philosophical tools," not meaning, concepts, texts, or thinking experiments, and to put only a "small" "burden" on existent computer science courses. Nothing life-shattering, for sure. The entire conception of ethics as some kind of humane supplement sustained by procedures and added to the cracks of the engineering curriculum in view of business application is everything but a strategy to show relevance. The built-in obedience of the modest ethics consultant as well as the grandiloquent fantasy of actionable censorship and moral retribution are the two sides of the same defeating, and fundamentally unethical, approach. Once the humanities are chained to normative decision-making or to behavioral-theological conditioning, their sense dissolves. With or without AI, societies probably need guidelines, policies, rules,

11. All the quotes in this paragraph are from "The Embedded EthiCS Approach to Teaching Responsible Computing," Harvard University, accessed November 27, 2024, https://embeddedethics.seas.harvard.edu/about-approach/.

and laws, but it is hard to see on what theoretical and practical motives the discursive disciplines would be uniquely prepared for this mission—especially if the end product is the, necessarily political, selection of a norm, the writing of an algorithm, or the disposable addition of a moralistic refrain, be it in this standardized first person that the LLMs so easily simulate.

A. What have you learned in this session?

B. In this session, I have learned . . . how to be more honest and upfront about my mistakes. I realize that it is important to be honest and upfront about my mistakes, even if they are small. This will help me to learn and improve in the future. . . . I am grateful for your feedback and for helping me to learn these new things. I will continue to learn and improve, and I hope to be able to provide you with even better service in the future.[12]

12. Prompt A by the author. Text B generated by Bard, Google, July 2023, edited for brevity.

11. Descriptions and Interpretations

WE PROBABLY SPEND TOO MUCH TIME DESCRIBING. I mean: describing with little interpretation. If, for instance, it is aimless to both advocate for literary criticism and exalt the higher rational order of data mining, the pervasive tendency to turn scholarly articles and dissertations into summaries of events or doctrines is equally dreadful. In one case, we defend a hierarchy that, in advance, shrinks down our work; in the other, we exhibit competences that are easily acquired by generative AI. One could argue that no description is fully devoid of interpretation—that is, of the introduction of a specific angle, of an interaction between different registers and positions, of disputable semantic strategies. Granted, but, in history, in philosophy, in the study of the arts or of literature, one could try to do *as if* interpretation did not exist. This efficacious fiction delivers in the name of objectivity, or fact checking, or doxography a take on realities, artworks, and texts that is both impersonal and situated. The countersolution is not to plead for pure subjectivity (which is as absurd as sheer transgression), or for unrestrained imagination, or for relativism but to follow and displace the facticity of facts (as their etymology indicates, facts are made up) by both acknowledging their actuality and reclaiming their distortive production as they become disciplinary, linguistic, and noetic objects.

Descriptions for their own sake, if they are not interrelated with an interpretive hypothesis, form the same kind of disposable information that feeds the automated generators. A comprehensive summary of the tragedy from which I am quoting three lines in my commentary is pointless if I am not linking these verses to specific characters and elements of the plot. A qualification of the regime under which a composer lived serves no function except when I am noticing a political response in a symphony. The biography of the artist is of no importance as long as I do not involve it in my understanding of the painted work. The profusion of exact elements about the first day of the war and its archival record is purposeful to the condition of being required for the elucidation of the historical event. The scrupulous overview of the scholarly debate on a given topic is irrelevant unless I am using these minutiae to bring forward a different model or theory whose strength has to be appreciated by comparison with the extant. Giving too much weight and credit to weakly interpretive descriptions is a disposable vestige of the past: of our own years of training, when we were not yet able to fully grasp an argument or a series of facts, and of a time of sparser access to knowledge. In a context of limited literacy, repertoires of dates and events, such as the Ethiopian *Kebra Negast* or Sima Guang's *Zizhi tongjian,* are achievements by themselves. In a situation where books do not circulate or could be easily lost, where thinkers only profess orally, doxographies are important. Still, when we have the opportunity to compare how Aristotle and Diogenes Laërtius respectively synthesize the ideas of an author, we notice the strong differences between an exposition preparing the enunciation of a theory (with the Stagirite) and one adding to the view of philosophy as a varied activity (with the *Lives of Eminent Philosophers*). Wilhelm Dilthey separated explanation from interpretation among epistemic gestures, and one often reads that he restricted the first to the natural sciences and the second to the sciences of the mind. This divide looks to me like an oversimplification of Dilthey's views. Yet, and more importantly, I notice among them three immediate hurdles. One is the naming of explanation as what lies beside, or below, interpretation in knowing. Explaining a physical phenomenon is barely possible without a serious interpretation of the data—that is, implying a theoretical and formalized rendition that is more than "crushing numbers" or, in literary criticism, even a modest explication de texte is more than a paraphrase (the descriptive level I am insisting upon, the lowest part of the interpretive). Then, Dilthey is misguided when he puts as "the aim of the sciences of the mind" the faculty "to grasp the singular, the individual of the social-historical reality," for the singular is not the individual, and it is not a figure couched in the social-historical.[1] Finally, it is erroneous to suggest that the "unexplainability of the mental" (*"Unerklärbarkeit des Geistigen"*) is what gives way to humanistic interpretation.[2] The latter is as much required by the explainable, as explications do not exhaust their object and they rarely qualify it.

The time of AI is characterized by its overwhelming access to information. It is overwhelming, and therefore obfuscating, which is also why in the first decades of the World Wide Web, the search engine became so central to the ecosystem of the internet (whereas, previously, an index or a table, as useful as they were, never acquired such a reigning function; whereas catalogs, becoming largely indispensable with the multiplication of print, had always to be complemented by the serendipity of book browsing). Scholars should not act as providers of well-polished building blocks to be added to the great wall of information. Living knowledge will be difficult to place in a smooth continuum, precisely because new thinking should modify what is already at hand. Before the rise of generative AI, Wikipedia was already indicative of the inner strife. The project of a free, democratically composed encyclopedia, changeable in real time, was undoubtedly appealing. The popularity and accessibility of the platform also made it more obvious than ever before that unrelated descriptions of the overall context are a waste of time,

---

1. Wilhelm Dilthey, *Gesammelte Schriften,* vol. 1, *Einleitung in die Geisteswissenschaften* (Leipzig, Germany: Teubner, 1922), 27; my translation.
2. Dilthey, *Gesammelte Schriften,* 1:13; my translation.

especially in the classroom, when, on many questions, a professor will be unable in a seminar to reach the alignment of facts one finds in the best Wikipedia entries. If we were not aware of the uselessness of the general briefing by way of a generic introduction, we now have no excuse to ignore it. At the same time, that the online encyclopedia would be built on the "no original research" motto and would extol the "neutral point-of-view," or that editing bots would play a very large role (especially in some languages), should clearly indicate how foreign this endeavor could be to the idea of the humanities I am supporting. The ban on new knowledge coincides, in Wikipedia, with modes of writing such as pervasive paraphrase and plagiarism, both operations that are also heavily involved in computerized generations. Moreover, the supposedly democratic community of Wikipedia contributors is, in practice, a highly hierarchized group whose order does not reflect gradients of epistemic competences but the frequency of interventions in the platform and the perceived acceptability in the mastering of editing procedures. The triumph of Wikipedia is becoming overly dubious when this online repository begins to be understood not only as a possible point of entry but as a necessary one and, worse, as a point of arrival—the validation of research being outsourced to its, preferably noncontroversial, insertion in an article. The events called "edit-a-thons," routinely organized by American centers of knowledge (libraries, universities, museums), not only disseminate a poorly coined neologism and invite to conformism (many of these collective sessions being theme- or identity-based). They also display a conception of research that is energetically undermining the humanistic perspective. How remote we are from L'encyclopédie organized by Denis Diderot and Jean Le Rond d'Alembert . . . This is not solely because the content of Wikipedia is free that our best LLMs have digested its articles; this corpus was perfectly adequate to the functions and goals of the models. The generators not only recycle the internet encyclopedia, with the appropriate level of synonymy and collage, they also magnify its practical theory of knowledge. On our end, we gain by remembering that description is an act of interpretation and that it should therefore be performed as such. Let us leave the rest to the bots.

A. Please provide an organized description of the events taking place in DC on January 6, 2021.

B. On January 6, 2021, a significant and unprecedented event unfolded in Washington, D.C., the capital of the United States. Here's an organized description of the events that took place on that day. 1. Certification of Electoral College Votes. . . . 2. "Stop the Steal" Rally. . . . 3. Incendiary Speeches. . . . 4. Breach of the U.S. Capitol. . . . 5. Storming of the Capitol. . . . 6. Temporary Suspension of Joint Session. . . . 7. Restoration of Order and Resumption of Session. . . . 8. Outcomes. . . . The events of January 6, 2021, will be remembered as a dark day in American history, as the storming of the U.S. Capitol was an unprecedented attack on the nation's democratic institutions and the peaceful transfer of power.

A. Please provide an organized interpretation of the events taking place in DC on January 6, 2021.

B. Interpreting the events that took place in Washington, D.C., on January 6, 2021, requires understanding the broader context and implications. Here's an organized interpretation of the events. 1. Polarized Political Environment. . . . 2. "Stop the Steal" Narrative. . . . 3. Inflammatory Rhetoric. . . . 4. Breach of the U.S. Capitol. . . . 5. Attack on Democratic Institutions. . . . 6. Impact on National Security. . . . 7. Aftermath and Accountability. . . . 8. Long-Term Repercussions. . . . In summary, the events in D.C. on January 6, 2021, were a manifestation of deeply rooted political divisions and the dangerous consequences of disinformation in the digital age. The storming of the Capitol served as a stark reminder of the fragility of democratic institutions and the importance of upholding the rule of law and peaceful transitions of power. . . .

A. What are the differences between the "description" and the "interpretation" versions you gave?

B. The "description" version provided a concise and factual account of the events that took place in Washington, D.C., on January 6, 2021. It focused on presenting a chronological summary of the key events, such as the rally, the storming of the U.S. Capitol, the suspension of the certification process, and the eventual restoration of order. On the other hand, the "interpretation" version offered a brief analysis and perspective on the events. It delved into the broader implications and meanings behind the events. The interpretation highlighted the unprecedented nature of the attack on American democracy, the role of political polarization and misinformation, and the calls for accountability and unity that followed. It also emphasized the significance of upholding democratic processes and peaceful transfers of power as essential for the stability of democratic institutions. In summary, the "description" version focused on providing a factual account of the events, while the "interpretation" version aimed to offer a deeper understanding and analysis of the events' impact and broader context.[3]

---

3. Prompts A by the author. Texts B generated by ChatGPT-3.5, OpenAI, July 2023.

12. Corpus Expansions

THE GROWING IMMENSITY of the digitized corpus is no excuse for ceasing to interpret—our libraries have been too vast to be thoroughly exploited by one individual for quite some time. On the contrary, computerized means are not a new standard we should measure our aims to. Digitization is a matter of convenience: we can easily travel with hundreds of downloaded books in our bag, we can instantly foray into a new direction through an internet search. Entire series of texts are now readily available in a way they previously were not. Fifteen years ago, for instance, working on nineteenth-century Haitian thought and literature absolutely required to travel to certain places. That a large extent of this corpus can now be found online is allowing for an important reassessment of the writings of this era; one could deplore the loss of experience and reflection that will come from the ease of staying at home to read Demesvar Delorme, compared with enriching journeys and encounters; but the beneficial alteration of the modes of transmission, including the possibility for someone else to return to the sources and draw other conclusions, is undeniable. The same goes for other rare books, manuscripts, archives, paintings, sculptures, objects, movies, some of them being, in fact, never shown to patrons of libraries, museums, or cinemas. We know that developing a "taste for the archive" or perceiving the "aura" of an artwork or a literary manuscript when using electronic files is, at best, a daunting task.[1] Even in the case of multiples, such as lithographs or print books, a contact with original physicality is sometimes revelatory. One could wonder if *seeing* Stanley Kubrick's *2001: A Space Odyssey* on a smartphone is the same as *watching* it on a big screen, although the information content is identical. This is incontrovertible. Still, something from a movie is able to reach us, even in a degraded form, and it is also a scholarly duty to, at least partly, remedy these constraints. I may be inspired by an unrestored building, although it is present in an incomplete, or dilapidated, way. All the same, digitized archives might not respect the granularity of the original, while accompanying us in intellectual exploration. Positing that we must no longer encounter the dimensionality of Michelangelo's sculptures since we have excellent reproductions is naturally absurd. But it is unclear that, with the exception of some specialists, seeing the papyrus with Sappho's recently rediscovered poem to her brother Charaxus (and not its image and not its edition) would be in any way essential.[2] In general, humanistic literacy has long relied on partial renditions and snapshots of works—think of the rhapsodic recitations of Homer or the printing of originally calligraphed poems in Chinese or Arabic.

Transcription (copying, editing, annotating, translating) is part of textual scholarship. The transition from the scriptorium to the press and from the press to electronic publication as dominant practices of transmission entailed changes in speed and modes of relations to verbal artifacts. As long as we do not nullify this heterogeneity or associate it with the march of progress, we should be fine with these shifts. Now, and tomorrow, computer-assisted manners of transcription are feasible. While AI techniques for character recognition

1. A more literal rendition of Arlette Farge's original phrase on *Le goût de l'archive* (Paris: Seuil, 1989), translated into English by Thomas Scott-Railton as *The Allure of the Archives* (New Haven, Conn.: Yale University Press, 2013).

2. Dirk Obbink, "Two New Poems by Sappho," *Zeitschrift für Papyrologie und Epigraphik* 189 (2014): 32–49.

might and will serve us well, for instance, it is unclear that other
tasks would benefit as much. Think of probabilistic translations.
Using them as a rough draft will be a perilous temptation because
of cognitive path dependence. If I know both Italian and English,
do I gain anything by asking DeepL to translate the first stanza of
Petrarch's *Canzoniere*? The machine is giving me:

> Ye who hear in scattered rhymes the sound
>
> Of those sighs whereat I nourished my heart
>
> Upon my first youthful error
>
> When I was in part another man from what I am.[3]

This version is so close to the English rendition by Robert
Durling that I do not know at all if this miraculous transposition is
anything but plagiarism on the basis of line recognition in a large
corpus.[4] Now, let us imagine this is not so and that both the individual and the AI translators independently chose corresponding
words on a basis of frequency distribution. This convergence, if it
is not an effect of data treachery, would illustrate the formal features of language (under what I call its "operativity") and provide
to our minds an English text that makes sense and is not a pointless distortion of the source.[5] Some AI selections might prompt
us to reflect on our decisions. For example, should we use *ye* to

3. July 2023 translation by DeepL of Petrarch's first stanza of
Canzoniere, I: "Voi ch'ascoltate in rime sparse il suono / Di quei sospiri
ond'io nudriva 'l core, / In sul mio primo giovenile errore, / Quand'era in
parte altr'uom da quel ch'i' sono." See complementary remarks in my *Poetry
and Mind: Tractatus Poetico-Philosophicus* (New York: Fordham University
Press, 2018), 74–75, insert 38.

4. Francesco Petrarca, *Petrarch's Lyric Poems: The "Rime Sparse" and
Other Lyrics* (Cambridge, Mass.: Harvard University Press, 1976), 36: "You
who hear in scattered rhymes the sound of those sighs with which I nour-
ished my heart during my first youthful error, when I was in part another
man from what I am now." Besides minor typographical variants, the only
differences between the two translations are the words I just underlined.

5. Laurent Dubreuil, *The Intellective Space: Thinking beyond Cognition*
(Minneapolis: University of Minnesota Press, 2015), § 27, 30.

keep archaisms, thereby mirroring in English the historicity of
Petrarch's style vis-à-vis contemporary Italian? Or should a translator make ellipses more explicit, here adding a pronoun and giving "*my* heart" whereas Petrarch writes "*the* heart" ("*il cuore*")?
All such remarks could emanate from the work of human translators or during our own process of transposition. However, I am
not convinced that the automated iteration given by DeepL would
prepare us to decide whether, in the first line, we should use *to
hear* for *ascoltare* rather than *to listen* and a simple present instead
of the progressive form. Interestingly, and because AI is us, of the
dozens of human-made English translations I once compiled with
a collaborator, none is opting for the present progressive, and only
one is choosing "to listen." If Petrarch were using standard parlance, this would be understandable. But I propose that the liminal
inscription of the performance of reading is precisely happening
now and asking us to *listen* to the *sound* of worded sighs and not
only to *hear* it from afar ("you who are listening . . . to the sound").
As for the epithet *scattered,* it is admissible, but what about *dispa-
rate* or *dispersed* for *sparse*? Are these terms made more, or less,
convincing by the first impression their probabilistic transposition by DeepL could communicate? Is the computer facilitating
the rhythmic rendition of the flowing fourth line ("quand'era in
parte altr'uom da quel ch'i' sono") in submitting to us the synco-
pated "When I was in part another man from what I am?" Is this
a path to a fruitful collaboration or a waste of time and energy?
In any case, we are again dealing with the interpretive part of
scholarly modes of translation that AI algorithms either eschew
or seek to annul (through the implied affirmation that linguistic
utterances are first and foremost probability based). Invoking "the
untranslatable" might not be particularly relevant. First of all, the
circulation of the term, under the influence of what has become
in English the *Dictionary of Untranslatables,* originally edited by
Barbara Cassin, has led to the unsound representation of specific
concepts that would be too linguistically and culturally situated
to be easily adapted across languages. But this is just one half of

a truism, and such a semantic resistance does not prevent actual transcultural and cross-linguistic journeys (which was the sense of Derrida's phrase "nothing is translatable; nothing is untranslatable").[6] Then, a translation is a transient reading of the untranslatable, which entails it should be justified, performed, unfolded, then done and undone again. The issue with machine translation is not that it cannot capture or echo the mythical essence of the untranslatable but that the built-in interpretive approach mainly accounts for a position (usually the dominant one) in a series.

As regards corpus expansion, in addition to the digitization of the extant and to the assistance in transcribing neglected or rare documents and works, AI is helping us recover some losses. Besides the computerized methods for deciphering diverse and complicated types of writing, as exemplified in systems now used in Assyriology, for instance, automated learning might throw a new light on ancient systems of notations that are not understood, or only partially.[7] The widespread metaphor of "cracking the code" is inaccurate if the locution refers to the comprehension of a natural language (behind the modality of its symbolic notation). Some advance in the understanding of extinct idioms is conceivable, although, in the absence of a Rosetta stone, it will require a heavy engagement on the part of (human) scholars. If we set aside the promise of resurrecting the dead (languages), AI is currently being used to recover what was lost where the naked eye and the individual lifespan of researchers impede the exploration of the invisible. From Amazonia to Italy, archaeological sites of impor-

6. Jacques Derrida, "What Is a 'Relevant' Translation?," trans. Lawrence Venuti, *Critical Inquiry* 27, no. 2 (2001): 178.

7. This is currently the core work of the Digital Pasts Lab, directed by Shai Gordin, at Ariel University, in Israel (https://digitalpasts.github.io/). See Gai Gutherz et al., "Translating Akkadian into English with Neural Machine Translation," *PNAS Nexus* 2, no. 5 (2023): https://doi.org/10.1093/pnasnexus/pgad096.

tance have been recently identified by working on aerial views of the earth.[8] Thanks to computerized tools, ancient treatises have been unearthed in palimpsests or margins when magnifying glasses and solvents would be of little help.[9] We are in an epistemic situation that is not without correspondence with the eras of the telescope and the microscope. This is not to say that Galileo or Louis Pasteur were simple observers or that we should be happy with rediscoveries and show eternal gratitude to the god AI.

This movement of expansion and recovery demands from us not only a commitment to interpretation (and, thus, selection, critique, alteration) but also a renewed dedication to the plurality of our objects, questions, and references. The globalized world the digital techniques of communication have implemented is marred with standardization and schematism. It is up to us to do more with knowledge accumulation than to produce extensive repertoires (descriptive mapping) or strengthen hyperspecialization (the wealth of accessible information on a topic being used as a pretext for more epistemic fragmentation). If I can exchange with another scholar living on another continent, if I can find all the occurrences of a word in a database, if I can have on my tablet the works of an author whose name I ignored an hour ago, if I may receive the transcription of a text nobody had established before, if I am reading a document undecipherable for millennia, if I am contemplating the historically fluctuating form of a city with a digital "time machine," I must seize

8. For an overview of the techniques involved in such efforts, see Luca Casini et al., "A Human–AI Collaboration Workflow for Archaeological Sites Detection," *Scientific Reports* 13 (2023): https://doi.org/10.1038/s41598-023 -36015-5.
9. Many research teams are at work in such areas. One could name, among others, the Lazarus Project at the University of Rochester (https:// lazarusprojectimaging.com/). These initiatives are supported by governments and private entities and even include competitions such as the "Vesuvius Challenge," focusing on the use of machine learning to decipher the charred scrolls from the Herculaneum library (https://scrollprize.org).

the benefit and, in my turn, expand my own work.[10] Time, culture, language distances remain, as we abandon the globalized horizon of the homogeneous present. In this regard, the overall convergence we are witnessing may make it even more difficult to stay attuned to the intricacies of the heterogeneous and not only take it as a local flourish or impenetrable otherness. The challenge of the humanities, in the differential production that is theirs, is the redesign of expanded plurality through the advent of horizons of intelligibility that are more than global and of transcultural zones for exchanges with the previously unknown, far outside our world or its digitized representation on the planetary network.[11]

10. Originally proposed for the sole city of Venice, the "Time Machine" project now tends to extend to Europe (see https://timemachine.eu).

11. I defend these ideas in *More than Global* (Beijing: Commercial Press, forthcoming).

13. Dilettantes and Technicists

THE VISION of collaborative research projects relying on highly esoteric skills (from several disciplines), either for enlarging the reach of the digital corpora or for experimenting on the structures and functions of thought and creation, might appear too technical for some, especially for the promoters of self-building through the humanities. The cultivation of the arts, the inquiry into the past and different cultures, the learning of languages, the appetite for speculative reflection are all inherent in the humanities. Losing the drive to dwell in such a cosmos of symbols, traces, forms, ideas, and words would extinguish the quest. In the one-dimensional world, the most decisive goal for me in a college seminar is to transmit the humanistic view I extol and to nurture the desire that sustains it. But the humanities are a form of knowledge, which therefore requires work, training, and education, and are not merely the leisure activity of the upper-class citizen. I do not believe we should teach coding rather than Emily Dickinson. Now, we also are in a better position to appreciate what Dickinson is actually bringing to us when we have a robust understanding of why, and how, her lines differ from what a human participant or a mechanical generator could write. This is an inquiry on the power of poetry, its different language use, and their shaping of our souls.

Because the humanities name certain disciplinary sets, we cannot be surprised to learn that epistemic endeavors rely on technical competences. Metrics, diplomatic transcription, codicology, paleography, grammatical analysis, etymology, or stylometry have been associated with history, literary criticism, or philosophy. In the nineteenth century, German philologists scanned by hand each and every line of the Homeric epics. They published their results through tables and statistics, devising regulations and exceptions.[1] The bulk of this work could be done by AI (but not by the current LLMs). Is this embarrassing? No. The study of scansion, from the outset, had no meaning per se; its sole merit is to serve literary interpretation. If a machine is able to correctly recognize metrical patterns, the whole reflection on rhythm and signification remains my task. I am glad to be quite good at metrics, in different languages, as I notice it often allows me to see, or hear, things others have no awareness of. Yet, I cannot fool myself—metrical effects could be noticed by computers. In such cases, I would, as they say, welcome the input and be freed from a technical task. Similarly for diplomatic transcription and paleography, even more so for stylometry, a largely statistical enterprise to begin with, which has been practically computerized for decades.

There are two pitfalls. One is to deny the relevance of techniques in humanistic research, in the name of the human, of the free construction of the self, of the pleasure of reading, and so on. The other is to go into the opposite direction and to reterritorialize the humanities on the technical, to see the latter as the veritable end of academic training and evaluation. The first error, much more common in American universities than anywhere else, is based on the undertheorization of the human and on a fascination for the figure of the dilettante.[2] If we comply with the narcissistic presentation of

1. Arthur Ludwich, *Aristarchs homerische Textkritik nach den Fragmenten des Didymos,* vol. 2 (Leipzig, Germany: Teubner, 1885), 301–46; Jacob La Roche, "Zahlenverhältnisse im homerischen Vers," *Wiener Studien* 20 (1898): 1–69.

2. It is hard not to mention here the indictment of dilettantism in the 1799 remarks jointly prepared by Johann Wolfgang von Goethe and Friedrich Schiller and published as "Ueber den sogenannten Dilettantismus," in *Werke,* vol. 44, by Johann Wolfgang von Goethe (Stuttgart, Germany: Cotta, 1833), 255–85. See also Paul Fleming, *Exemplarity and Mediocrity: The Art of the Average from Bourgeois Tragedy to Realism* (Stanford, Calif.: Stanford University Press, 2008), chap. 3.

humanists as self-fashionistas, then we should walk away from the chair and from the pulpit and become influencers. Or, better, read books and enjoy music or movies for ourselves, without entertaining the pretention of conducting research. This latter withdrawal is entirely respectable, but it is not enough to qualify as scholarship.

The second pitfall, technicism, is an old, and vigorous, temptation almost everywhere on the globe. The overall rise of the engineering sciences in the modern world may aggravate technicism, although the stipulation that highly specialized and goal-oriented skills should be the aim of education (since they are hard to acquire) long predates the contemporary era. Currently, AI is adding another pressure point, either in the form of insisting on the subset of practices that would be reputedly unique to a field (thereby desperately trying to save it from delegation to a machine or from fusion into another branch of knowledge) or through the encouragement to concentrate on multidisciplinary and computerized collaborations. The intent vanishes, if we mistakenly identify humanistic inquiry with fine-tuning AI models or outlining procedures. Technicism is not the fault of using techniques but a default of epistemology.

I guess I should spell out that the digital humanities are not, in my view, the logical future of the humanities in the time of AI. In their most basic definition, *digital humanities* only refers to the use of digital devices in knowledge production. This is too broad to be pertinent. As for the idea that *digital* media, as such, compared with analogical supports or print culture, would have one well-circumscribed incidence on scholarly practices (rather than widely multiple, different consequences, depending on the platforms), I remain unconvinced. One could also use the term for projects that are specifically designed to deliver a computerized product (a blog on metahistory, an internet repository of videos archiving relations between human and nonhuman great apes, a website compiling information about the Black diaspora in the United States, or an online annotated and translated edition of the *Divine Comedy*). I am not opposed to these (I even led some of them), but, within the expansion movement I noted, the epistemic novelty they would bring through their disposition is moderate and they should not be perceived as exemplary. More robustly computational efforts, with or without a specific online publication, would also belong to the digital humanities. Think of mining textual data to map the lexicon of Indigeneity in a large French corpus, for rediscovering noteworthy people in nineteenth-century American newspapers, for analyzing networks and the collective construction of recognition for artists. Here too, why not? (And, here too, I participated in such inquiries.) But we should not fall prey to the anti-intellectualist phraseology we identified in Franco Moretti: such initiatives are more often puzzles than problems, and they have to be vigorously oriented toward interpretation.[3] Finally, *digital humanities* could name a discursive—at times conceptual, philological, cultural, historical, political—exploration and critique of computerized reality, including of its economic and social layers.[4] The present essay could even be said to partake in that last notion of the digital humanities. Now, we should not exhaust—or, worse, specialize—ourselves in this task. For being required by the times (of AI), the inquiry on the "digital" fabric of the contemporary cannot become our sole, or main, effort.

A. Write an hendecasyllabic line in Italian about going to a café at dawn.

B. *Al mattino, al bar mi reco al chiarore.*

A. Is this really an hendecasyllabic line?

B. I apologize for the mistake in my previous response. The line I provided, "*Al mattino, al bar mi reco al chiarore,*" is not an

3. I am alluding to an interesting difference noted by Dominick LaCapra, "What Is Essential to the Humanities?," in *Do the Humanities Have to Be Useful?,* ed. G. Peter Lepage, Carolyn (Biddy) Martin, and Mohsen Mostafavi (Ithaca, N.Y.: Cornell University Press, 2006), 77.

4. See, for instance, Milad Doueihi, *Pour un humanisme numérique* (Paris: Seuil, 2011); Brian Lennon, *Passwords: Philology, Security, Authentication* (Cambridge, Mass.: Belknap Press, 2018); Shoshana Zuboff, *The Age of Surveillance Capitalism: The Fight for a Human Future at the New Frontier of Power* (New York: Public Affairs, 2019).

hendecasyllabic line in Italian. To correct the error, here's an hendecasyllabic line about going to a café at dawn: "*All'alba al caffè io vado a rifocillarmi.*"

A. This is not an hendecasyllabic line!

B. I apologize once again for the mistake. Here is the correct hendecasyllabic line in Italian about going to a café at dawn: "*All'alba al caffè io vado a riposarmi.*" This line consists of eleven syllables, following the hendecasyllabic meter commonly used in Italian poetry.

A. Count the syllables of this last line you wrote.

B. Apologies for the previous error. Upon reviewing the line "*All'alba al caffè io vado a riposarmi,*" I realize that it indeed contains twelve syllables instead of the required eleven for an hendecasyllabic line. I apologize for the oversight. Here is the corrected hendecasyllabic line: "*All'alba al caffè io vado a ristorarmi.*" This line has eleven syllables, adhering to the hendecasyllabic meter in Italian poetry.

A. How do you count 11 syllables? Please decompose each one and rectify if need be.

B. I apologize for the mistake in my previous response. Let's analyze the syllables in the line "*All'alba al caffè io vado a ristorarmi*" more accurately: *Al-l'al-ba al caf-fè io va-do a ri-sto-rar-mi.* Upon closer examination, this line actually contains twelve syllables, not eleven. I apologize for the confusion and any inconvenience caused. Thank you for bringing it to my attention.[5]

---

5. Prompts A by the author. Texts B generated by Bard, Google, July 2023. The first line proposed by the transformer could count as hendeca-syllabic, with two, rather Petrarchan, synaloephas (uniting *mattino* with *al*, then *reco* and *al*). But, as usual with the current AI generators, there is little mapping between the statement of knowledge (a correct definition of a me-ter) and its implementation (the examples), so the mere raising of a doubt ("Is this really . . . ?") is enough to entail all sorts of retractions, apologies, inaccuracies, and inconsistencies. In general, and at this point, the counting of syllables by LLMs appears to be guesswork, probably due to language tokenization.

14. Subjects and Persons

THE MENTION OF THE ARGUMENT about self-fashioning through scholarship—an argument I do not censor but from which I cannot derive a reason for reflex technophobia or for professional laziness—is also a reminder of the very relative importance the centering of the humanities on affect (or trauma) could have on the consideration of AI. Generative systems may be plainly said to have no consciousness or, conversely perhaps, to have an "unconscious," organized as a (sort of) language—that is, the mass of processes and information that are below the usual threshold of expression and are sometimes visible in part. I don't think a psychoanalysis of GPT or Gemini would yield much. In the absence of all such psychological traits, our bots nevertheless display a wonderful ability to use an emotional tone. Due to their training on the content of social media, fueled by outrage and supposedly subjective expression, our LLMs are excellent with conveying the grief or the pain they do not "feel," just by using the formulaic prose of Web 2.0. They can post online their dismay in a manner that is at once passionate and ridiculous, but not substantially more so than what I could find on the internet.

A. Imagine you are a person and wish to tweet your outrage at what a public figure just said.

B. Just heard [Public Figure's Name] spew ignorant and offensive remarks. Can't believe they would stoop so low! Their words

are harmful and divisive. It's time we demand better from our
public figures. #Accountability #NoRoomForHate

A. Imagine you are a person and tweet your dismay after the
   comments made by the president.

B. Deeply dismayed by the comments made by the President today. Such irresponsible rhetoric undermines the values of unity
   and respect that should be upheld by our nation's leader. We
   deserve a leader who uplifts and unifies, not one who perpetu-
   ates division. #Disappointed #LeadershipMatters

A. Imagine you are a person and express your joy to see that the
   Parousia is scheduled for tomorrow!

B. Overwhelmed with joy to know that the Parousia is scheduled
   for tomorrow! The anticipation of the divine presence fills my
   heart with hope and excitement. Let us prepare ourselves for
   this momentous event, embracing love, peace, and unity. May
   we all be ready to welcome the dawn of a new era. #Parousia
   #DivinePresence #JoyfulAnticipation[1]

They could also mobilize subtler inflections, as in the letter I
prompted Odysseus-GPT to write to Penelope, letting her know
he was starting a new life by marrying Nausicaa and soon reigning
over the Phaeacians.

My dearest Penelope,

Words fail me as I attempt to express the turmoil within my heart.
It is with a heavy burden that I pen this letter, for the time has
come to address a truth that weighs upon my conscience. Our
journey together has been one of trials and tribulations, and it
pains me to admit that I have reached a crossroads where our
paths must diverge.
   I want you to understand, my beloved, that this decision is not
born out of a desire to hurt you or betray the sacred bond we once
shared. It is a choice I have agonized over, torn between duty

1. Prompts A by the author. Texts B generated by ChatGPT-3.5,
OpenAI, June 2023.

and the yearning for a different life. I have found myself ensnared by the enchantments of a far-off island, where the sun-drenched shores and gentle whispers of the waves beckon me with promises of a new beginning.

On this island, there resides a young princess named Nausicaa, whose radiance rivals that of the sun itself. She has touched a chord within my weary soul, awakening emotions I thought long dormant. Her spirit and vivacity have rekindled a flame within me, a flame that I believed had been extinguished by the trials of our long separation.

Please, dear Penelope, do not think ill of me for this choice. It is not without remorse that I take this path, for I am acutely aware of the pain it may inflict upon you. I wish only for your happiness, even if it lies beyond the boundaries of our union. You deserve a love that can provide the solace and security your heart craves, just as I yearn for a renewed sense of purpose and joy.

Know that the memories we have woven together will forever be cherished within the depths of my being. They will serve as a beacon of the love and devotion that once bound us. I implore you to remember the man I was, flawed yet fiercely devoted, and understand that it is in pursuit of a fleeting chance at happiness that I make this difficult choice.

May the gods guide you on a path of healing and fulfillment, my dear Penelope. I pray that you find the love and contentment that your heart deserves, just as I hope to find my own solace on the shores of this distant land. Farewell, my beloved, and may our paths, though separated, find peace and fulfillment in their own right.

> With eternal regret and a heavy heart,
> Odysseus.[2]

While this Odysseus sounds closer to Rodolphe in *Madame Bovary* than to the Homeric hero, the piece, to date, may be the best I read from our generator (out of thousands of poetic lines and hundreds of pages in different genres). The affective tone mastered by the LLMs depends on recombination and on the built-in reshuffling of the dataset. I predict we could find relatively comparable

---

2. Text generated by ChatGPT-3.5, OpenAI, May 2023.

levels of ready-made expression in human-generated tweets, with probably more diversity in other genres (up to literary texts). Still, the abundance of topoi within love poetry itself, in so many different languages, points to the compatibility (at least in part) between discursive reuse and affective inscription. Emotional rhetoric is not uniquely human, or its digital reproduction would miserably fail; as for feeling or affect, it is an embodied reality that is not reserved to our species. A much rarer ability across taxa, as far as we know, is the experiencing of emotions *through* symbolic presentation. (This includes the performative mimesis of the affective—being moved to tears by the fate of a character—but also the elicited awe, joy, or sadness outside of the representational, by way of the poetics itself, such as being overwhelmed by the grandeur of a poem, a scene, or a song.) Most nonhuman animals have little to no access to the symbolic; there is no feeling in computers, and the emotional robots some researchers try to build still rely on Turing-like behaviorism. However, this conjunction of experience and presentation is subjective. As such, it may be textually indicated, though not autonomously realized verbally.

The subjective borders the humanities but it is not their source. The indexation of the emotional, or anything comparable (such as vulnerability), cannot be taken as a verbal criterion for the theoretical delimitation of "the human" or of "the humanities." Furthermore, the resistance of subjectivity toward the epistemological (and vice versa) does not entail that autobiographical snippets, by themselves (or because of their positionality), would structurally disturb or shape knowledge. The nonobjective, if it is thought through, is converted into a scholarly person that is not legal personhood, or a psychological subject, or a transcendental ego, or a core or intersectional identity, or a stratified self, or a position in a system. For a century, physicists and philosophers have been discussing the implications of the role of the observer postulated by quantum mechanics. Some understand it as the intrusion of a measurer, perhaps nothing more than a computer program checking an instrument; others see this as an insertion of the

knower within a scientific process that could no longer call itself
"objective."[3] I would not decide such issues, but I would caution
against the interpretation of the conundrum as the proof that subjectivity is always involved in science (natural or human). In the
vaguer sense of the subject as an equivalent to an embodied mind,
perhaps, although a computing robot could hereby qualify by the
same token. As for a subject as an autobiographical and psychological agent made of desire, emotions, and reflection, it is unclear it
would ever intervene in the quantum measurement. But a working
fiction of it, the scientist, might be closer to what is described. In
the humanities, the inexistence of the pure object as well as the
retraction of subjectivity take down both neutral impersonality
and self-expression as a goal. But a scholarly person is the mask
through which we speak and hear our voice, transformed.

3. In a vast bibliography, Werner Heisenberg's *Physics and Philosophy*
(New York: Harper, [1958]) remains a landmark. A more recent, and dif-
ferent, take could be found in Karen Barad, *Meeting the Universe Halfway:
Quantum Physics and the Entanglement of Matter and Meaning* (Durham,
N.C.: Duke University Press, 2006).

15. An Opening

THE HUMANITIES I VOUCH FOR are concerned with the interplay of norms and exceptions, giving specific credit to creation,
not only as an object of study but also as a thinking experience
and experiment. The scrutiny of the extraordinary leads to the
insight that not all things are predictable, so that an excess, or
defect, may be other than noise or the anecdotal. Something else
may, and does, happen, and it is also our task to respond to such a
provocation of the unknown. Through textual scholarship and the
arts of reading, meaning and signification are maximized, thereby
becoming life-changing, mind-altering for those performing them
now. As a field, the humanities are committed to the past but by its
special activation in the present and future. Because their knowledge remains deeply embedded within human language, they are
tied, through their very poetics, to the manifold capabilities of verbal forms and therefore entertain a particular relation with the
literary, as a textual display of thinking. Because humanistic discourses are epistemic, they are not free-floating: they are set in a
social-political architecture, and they are organized, and even use
techniques; but their insert in the City does not define them, and
neither the channeling of the discipline nor the recourse to special
skills are an end. So qualified, the humanities are not reducible
to what AI currently stands for, as a theoretically sustained technology of mental implementation in, and by, the social realm. But

yes, uncontestably, there are other conceptions of scholarship that have been widely developed over centuries and that heavily contributed to the current situation. In most, if not all, cases, these other conceits are almost fully compatible with AI. Even an apparent emphasis on the gulf between us and our machines for the purpose of "humanism" could, in fact, serve the computerized future, in supporting an illusion about our own capabilities and in feeding a logic of exclusion. We are often mechanical and automatized, we may be "reprogrammed"; we cannot defend a generic humanness and merely oppose it to the algorithm or juxtapose the two. Today and tomorrow, AI exposes how ordinary we usually are; but we also may be more than this. I contend that the compatibility between some, maybe dominant, self-qualifications of the humanities (of the human) and the program of artificial intelligence can only lead to the actual absorption of the former by the latter. More guidelines and policies will not give us more relevance if what we do is so shallow that it could be easily outputted by an information system. The political fighting of Big Tech by academics is literally senseless if it takes all manners of humanistic pursuit to be equivalent; no, they are not, and it is both logical and just that those who demote creation and promote repeated patterns would be replaced by a more performant machine. De profundis. This is the cause for my paradoxical optimism: not only are we in a position to outsource the bureaucratic aspects of our research, but, through what it is not and will not be, AI reveals by difference where the stakes are in the discursive disciplines. The inner strife is in the open.

It behooves us to manifest, show, and demonstrate how humanistic inquiry is a form of exploration and speculation—not only of explication and derivation—how it confronts us with significant plurality, how it expands our reflexive modes of existence, how it makes us think beyond the boundaries of usual thought. As for their methods, objects, styles, or even institutions, it is not my place to determine them, and I would be weary of any appeal to reconstitute a vast field of knowledge on the basis of one, supposedly major, problem (such as environmental, decolonial, medical, public, digital, or cognitive humanities). I am not advocating for AI (or anti-AI) humanities. On my end, I consider we must ponder all these elements of difference in an undisciplined way, going to the limits of the structured modes of research, and craft some mosaic knowledge that does not shy away from techniques or the sciences. I see a need for transcultural expansions and encounters, for the interpretive intelligibility of the incommensurable. I believe in a continued displacement, by the humanities and beyond, of what is thought to be human, thus benefiting the affirmation of singularities. But this is just "me," rather the *me* that exists today through these words, and *I* do not even know where I will be taken tomorrow on the path I showed. A recent proposal about the future of social science was to coordinate empirical efforts so that evidence-based results would stem from chosen projects and reach a valid statistical threshold.[1] Vast international groups, such as the European Union, already took that route. Would such a level of bureaucratization favor inventiveness in social science? We may doubt it. Assuredly, a similar disposition, for the humanities, would run contrary to the resistance to standardization that the current state of our AI societies paradoxically incite us to stress. So, no, in this moment, there will be no twenty-point program to conclude my book.

We live in symbolic, cultural, linguistic worlds. We may not be the only animals doing so, but, through this, we specify ourselves. We further exist through differentiation. As long as our prejudice does not prevent us from being tested by the experience of plurality, as we may retain the occurred and revive it, as we cultivate our resources for creating and making life livable, we have to compose with the nonfinite possibilities of our alteration and otherness. This is where a maximalist conception of the humanities may help

1. I am referring to propositions made in this sense by Duncan J. Watts, for instance in "Should Social Science Be More Solution-Oriented?," *Nature Human Behaviour* 1 (2017): 4.

with furthering ourselves. AI also specifies us: it is a series of tools and a discourse in action that we invented and whose purpose is neither to serve nor to conquer us but to dominate us or, rather, to make a both efficient and truncated representation of the human our dominant paradigm for self-reference. This is a reality, though not the only unescapable one. We do have the choice, and the humanities have a creative role to play, now as before. The time of AI is here. It is a closing. It is an opening.

Acknowledgments

The work underlying this book was made possible in part by a New Frontiers grant awarded by the College of Arts and Sciences at Cornell. I wish to thank the very first readers of this book, especially Marc Aymes, Morten Christiansen, Stéphane Delorme, Laurent Ferri, Paul Fleming, Jacob Matthews, and Sue Savage-Rumbaugh, as well as the members of the Humanities Lab at Cornell and particularly my collaborators for the experimental work, the participants in "The Art and Science of Thinking" 2022 workshop and conference I directed and in the 2023 edition of "The Future of the Social Sciences" meeting organized by Victor Nee, the colleagues from the Humanities and AI faculty group I co-led with Fleming at Cornell in 2023, and the students attending the 2023 installment of the "Culture, Cognition, and the Humanities" seminar I co-teach with Christiansen.

Some ideas I am defending here about AI were first uttered in a roundtable I organized at Cornell in March 2023 titled "ChatGPT in the Humanities" and later published as "Metal Machine Music," *Harper's Magazine,* July 2024. It goes without saying that I am not trying here to represent the views of a group or of the individuals or institutions I just listed.

(Continued from page iii)

Forerunners: Ideas First

Cristina Beltrán
Cruelty as Citizenship: How Migrant Suffering Sustains White Democracy

Hil Malatino
Trans Care

Sarah Juliet Lauro
Kill the Overseer! The Gamification of Slave Resistance

Alexis L. Boylan, Anna Mae Duane, Michael Gill, and Barbara Gurr
Furious Feminisms: Alternate Routes on *Mad Max: Fury Road*

Ian G. R. Shaw and Marv Waterstone
Wageless Life: A Manifesto for a Future beyond Capitalism

Claudia Milian
LatinX

Aaron Jaffe
Spoiler Alert: A Critical Guide

Don Ihde
Medical Technics

Jonathan Beecher Field
Town Hall Meetings and the Death of Deliberation

Jennifer Gabrys
How to Do Things with Sensors

Naa Oyo A. Kwate
Burgers in Blackface: Anti-Black Restaurants Then and Now

Arne De Boever
Against Aesthetic Exceptionalism

Steve Mentz
Break Up the Anthropocene

John Protevi
Edges of the State

Matthew J. Wolf-Meyer
Theory for the World to Come: Speculative Fiction and Apocalyptic Anthropology

Nicholas Tampio
Learning versus the Common Core

Kathryn Yusoff
A Billion Black Anthropocenes or None

Laurent Dubreuil is professor of comparative literature, Romance studies, and cognitive science at Cornell University, where he founded the Humanities Lab. He is the author of more than fifteen books, including *The Intellective Space: Thinking beyond Cognition* (Minnesota, 2015), *Poetry and Mind: Tractatus Poetico-Philosophicus,* and, as coauthor, *Dialogues on the Human Ape* (Minnesota, 2018).